Genealogical Research
for Czech and
Slovak Americans

GALE GENEALOGY AND LOCAL HISTORY SERIES

Series Editor: J. Carlyle Parker, Head of Public Services and Assistant Library Director, California State College, Stanislaus; and Founder and Librarian Volunteer, Modesto California Branch Genealogical Library of the Genealogical Department of the Church of Jesus Christ of Latter-day Saints, Salt Lake City, Utah

Also in this series:

AMERICAN INDIAN GENEALOGICAL RESEARCH—*Edited by Jimmy B. Parker and Noel R. Barton**

AN INDEX TO THE BIOGRAPHEES IN 19TH-CENTURY CALIFORNIA COUNTY HISTORIES—*Edited by J. Carlyle Parker**

BLACK GENESIS—*Edited by James Rose and Alice Eichholz*

BLACKS IN THE FEDERAL CENSUS—*Edited by James Rose and Alice Eichholz**

CITY, COUNTY, TOWN, AND TOWNSHIP INDEX TO THE 1850 FEDERAL CENSUS SCHEDULES—*Edited by J. Carlyle Parker**

COMPENDIUMS OF QUAKER GENEALOGICAL RESEARCH—*Edited by Willard Heiss**

GENEALOGICAL HISTORICAL GUIDE TO LATIN AMERICA—*Edited by Lyman De Platt**

GENEALOGICAL RECORDS OF BLACKS IN SOUTHEASTERN CONNECTICUT, 1650-1900—*Edited by James Rose and Barbara Brown**

LIBRARY SERVICE FOR GENEALOGISTS—*Edited by J. Carlyle Parker**

MENNONITE GENEALOGICAL RESEARCH—*Edited by Delbert Gratz**

MONTANA'S GENEALOGICAL RECORDS—*Edited by Dennis L. Richards**

A PERSONAL NAME INDEX TO ORTON'S "RECORDS OF CALIFORNIA MEN IN THE WAR OF THE REBELLION, 1861 TO 1867"—*Edited by J. Carlyle Parker*

A SURVEY OF AMERICAN GENEALOGICAL PERIODICALS AND PERIODICAL INDEXES—*Edited by Kip Sperry*

WESTERN CANADIAN GENEALOGICAL RESEARCH—*Edited by Jimmy B. Parker and Noel R. Barton**

*in preparation

General Editor: Paul Wasserman, Professor and former Dean, School of Library and Information Services, University of Maryland

Managing Editor: Denise Allard Adzigian, Gale Research Company

Genealogical Research for Czech and Slovak Americans

Volume 2 in the Gale Genealogy and Local History Series

Olga K. Miller

formerly Research Consultant
LDS Genealogical Library
Salt Lake City, Utah

Gale Research Company
Book Tower, Detroit, Michigan 48226

Library of Congress Cataloging in Publication Data

Miller, Olga K
    Genealogical research for Czech and Slovak Americans.

    (Gale genealogy and local history series ; v. 2)
    Includes index.
    1. Czechoslovakia--Genealogy--Handbooks, manuals, etc.
2. Genealogy. I. Title.
CS524.M54   929'.1'09437   78-13086
ISBN 0-8103-1404-5

VITA

Olga Komárková Miller was born in Brno, Czechoslovakia. She emigrated to the United States where she raised four children. She was a research consultant at the LDS Genealogical Library and specialized in research in the United States, Canada, and Czechoslovakia. In addition to publishing numerous articles in professional journals, Miller has published MIGRATION, EMIGRATION AND IMMIGRATION.

CONTENTS

Contents

MAPS AND TABLES

Maps

Tables

FOREWORD

Those facing the linguistic, historical, and political complexities of Czech genealogical research will be most happy about the appearance of Olga Miller's GENEALOGICAL RESEARCH FOR CZECH AND SLOVAK AMERICANS. She presents a well-ordered procedure for dealing with these complexities and has skillfully summarized insights gained through many years of research experience.

After a general discussion of the historical and geographical aspects of genealogical research, the author turns her attention to a detailed presentation of research done in Czechoslovakia. The first problem to be solved is the identification of the family's first immigrant ancestor in America. Miller spends considerable time discussing the patterns of immigration to the United States from Czechoslovakia and the sources which must be used to identify the original immigrant. The next two chapters are devoted to various aspects of research in Czechoslovakia itself. In my opinion, the fifth chapter is by far the most significant. In this chapter the importance of vital records, parish registers, census returns, military records and land records in genealogical research are all discussed in great detail. The location and availability of these sources are topics also covered here.

Unfortunately, many people of Czech ancestry have not retained a knowledge of their forefathers' language. The author has, therefore, provided language material along with extensive lists of names, abbreviations, and a glossary of terms frequently encountered in analyzing Czech documents. A discussion of the various scripts used throughout the development of Czech record keeping is also provided. Sufficient material is given to assist the researcher in making a determination of the importance of the document being used.

Though GENEALOGICAL RESEARCH FOR CZECH AND SLOVAK AMERICANS can be read profitably from cover to cover, its most efficient application will be as a research tool, used selectively to overcome thorny research problems. Each chapter is autonomous and concludes with an extensive bibliography. The concise list of archives, sources, names, and abbreviations will be most beneficial to the novice and expert alike.

Foreword

Everywhere evident in this book is Olga Miller's deep, abiding love and concern for her native land. GENEALOGICAL RESEARCH FOR CZECH AND SLOVAK AMERICANS will prove to be a source of strength and knowledge to all those who are fortunate enough to have ancestral lines in Czechoslovakia.

Dr. Dennis B. Neuenschwander

PREFACE

With the completion of this work I feel both relief and con-
tentment. I would hope that my effort reflects the accumu-
lated knowledge and love of the work I have acquired through
many years of genealogical research. I humbly dedicate it
to all Americans of Czech ancestry, and I trust it will
serve well all who read it.

I have included a short history of the Republic, convinced
that it is both necessary and helpful in understanding the
people of Czechoslovakia and their record-keeping practices.
The subject of geography is also included because of its
importance in successful genealogical research. A considerable amount of information concerning the complexity of
Czech and Slovak names and a thorough explanation of possible Czech and Slovak sources for finding genealogical data
have also been given. I have written briefly concerning the
language and grammar, fully realizing the limitations of my
instructions. I have compiled in a glossary the most frequently used Czech genealogical terms; a list of calendar
days; and a comparative list of Czech, Slovak, Latin, German,
and English given names, all of which will be helpful in
Czech genealogical research.

Following each chapter is a comprehensive bibliography of
sources, including books, microfilms, periodicals, articles,
and lectures. Some of these I examined personally. Many,
however, were not available to me. Books or microfilms
contained in the holdings of the Genealogical Library of
the Church of Jesus Christ of Latter-Day Saints are indicated for each source by listing the initials GL and the call
number. By using the services of the Genealogical Library's
branches, most of the microfilm holdings can be attained
through a loan for a small service fee. The books held by
the Genealogical Library do not circulate on interlibrary
loan, but may be consulted through the use of a library
reference questionnaire.

The books and periodicals that have been published in
Czechoslovakia and are not in the Genealogical Library can
be obtained through the services of ARTIA (Prague I, Ve
Smečkách 30, Czechoslovakia) or through book dealers either
in America, London, Berlin, or Vienna. The annotations in

the bibliographies evaluate these sources for their useful-
ness in genealogical research.

My severe but kind critic was Dr. Dennis Neuenschwander,
Slavic area specialist at the Genealogical Library, to whom
I am very grateful for seeing errors in style or arrange-
ment that escaped my attention.

As this is the first attempt at compiling a Czechoslovakian
genealogical handbook written for Americans, the reader no
doubt will find errors. Possibly books and articles, perhaps whole journals, have been overlooked, either by commission or omission. In which case, I apologize in advance
and encourage any user to forward relevant information for
any future editions of this bibliography.

Olga K. Miller

Chapter 1

THE GENEALOGICAL LIBRARY OF THE CHURCH OF JESUS CHRIST OF LATTER-DAY SAINTS

Throughout the text of the book this library is referred to merely as the Genealogical Library and, in the bibliographies, abbreviated as GL.

The Genealogical Library is a division of the Genealogical Department of the Church of Jesus Christ of Latter-Day Saints. Founded in 1894 to comply with the religious beliefs of the Latter-Day Saints Church, the library's purpose was to make the genealogical source material available to the members of the church in searching out the records of their ancestors. Very soon after its founding, however, the holdings of the library were made available to everyone, regardless of church affiliation. At present, all are welcome to use the library without entrance or rental fee for any of the books or films.

From its beginning in 1894, with 100 books, the Genealogical Library has grown into an institution that is the largest of its kind in the world. The Genealogical Department of the church is involved in a worldwide microfilming program wherein records of genealogical value are microfilmed and sent to the Genealogical Library and stored there. While the holdings of the library include only 147,000 volumes, the total reels of microfilm exceed 1 million (equivalent to 4,180,000 volumes of about 300 pages each).

Priority in the acquisition of microfilmed records has been given to those areas of the world from which there has been heavy immigration to the United States. Consequently, the Genealogical Library has extensive records from Holland, the Scandinavian countries (Denmark, Norway, Finland, Sweden, and Iceland), and parts of Great Britain. There are current microfilming projects in South America, Canada, Mexico, Germany, France, Belgium, and Austria. Of all the Eastern European countries, only Hungary and Poland have given their consent to the microfilming program. Negotiations are in progress in other countries in Eastern Europe. It is impossible to predict when permission will be granted by these countries. To those who are sincerely interested, I suggest that they periodically contact the nearest branch of the Genealogical Library to inquire about the status of negotiations. At the end of this book, there is a list of branch libraries with their locations and exact addresses. Since new branch libraries are constantly being added, the most current information concerning branch locations can be obtained from the Genealogical Library (50 East North Temple, Salt Lake City, Utah 84103).

Branch libraries can supply their patrons with the microfilmed copies of all unrestricted records deposited in the main library. The fee is nominal, with the microfilm copies to be used on the premises of the libraries. The services of the branch libraries are also available to anyone. Thus, the source among the library's holdings referred to in the bibliographies throughout this book are available in any part of the United States where there is a branch library.

While waiting for permission to microfilm genealogical records in Czechoslovakia, the Genealogical Library is purchasing all nonrestricted books, periodicals, brochures, maps, gazeteers, and guides that may be of help in preparing for genealogical research in the Republic. Their value and use has been explained in various chapters throughout the book. There are libraries in the United States that have considerably larger numbers of books in the Czech language in their possession (such as the Chicago Public Library, New York Public Library, and many public libraries in Nebraska and Texas); however, none of them has more material significant for genealogical research than does the Genealogical Library.

The following enumeration will help the reader take full advantage of the services of the Genealogical Library. There is no charge for most of these services:

A. Expert assistance is provided in the use of the card catalog and indexes. (Mail requests for photocopies of specific parts of the card catalog are honored.) Advice on research problems and procedures is also available.

B. General mail inquiries are answered although detailed research in books and firms cannot be done.

C. A list of private genealogists accredited for research in the records is available and will be sent to anyone on request. State the country of interest.

D. Survey service is provided to help patrons determine whether others have collected and submitted information on a given ancestral line. Suggestions on extending the line can be given. A pedigree chart indicating the surname of interest should be submitted along with $10.

E. Copy Service:
   1. At library: books $.05 a sheet; films $.15 a sheet.
   By mail: books $.15 a sheet; films $.25 a sheet.

2. The Genealogical Library has a collection of over seven million family group records. These records have been submitted by both members and nonmembers of the Latter-Day Saints Church. They are arranged in alphabetical order. Copy service is available for a small fee and a $.50 fee is charged for mail requests to search.

3. In the Index Bureau, a division of the Genealogical Library, over 30 million individual index cards are alphabetized phonetically by the surname. Here searches are made by trained personnel. No information will be given on individuals possibly still living. There is a small charge for the forms for this service, plus a $.50 service fee for each request.

4. In the Computer File Index there are over 28 million names from many countries and periods of time. Entries are alphabetical by country. Most of the branch libraries have copies of this index.

The Genealogical Library also has on film the baptismal books and priesthood ordinations of the former Czechoslovakian Latter-Day Saints Mission from 1928-42. The mission had branches in Bohemia at Prague, Mladá Boleslav, Kosmonosy, Mnichovo Hradiště, Pardubice, Plzeň and in Moravia at Brno, Olomouc, and Prostějov. The mission presidents were: Arthur Gaeth, Wallace F. Toronto, and Josef Roubíček.

All records containing data on individuals still living are restricted. They cannot be reproduced for use in the branch libraries and can be searched only by authorized accredited researchers. No data found in the mission records can be photo-reproduced. If any member of the Latter-Day Saints Church wishes to obtain a copy of his baptismal certificate, he should write to the church's history department (50 East North Temple, Salt Lake City, Utah 84103). The original books of the Czechoslovakian mission are deposited there. The Genealogical Library is not authorized to verify and authenticate any data found in these books or films.

The books and periodicals within the holdings of the Genealogical Library in Salt Lake City may be consulted in part by completing a "Reference Questionnaire" at any one of the branch libraries. Questions must be concise and not involve lengthy research for answers. Examples of questions that can be successfully asked by this means are those concerning the identification of the district in which a town is located and requests to check an index for a specific family surname.

Chapter 2
HISTORY

A successful genealogical researcher needs to be acquainted with the customs of the people and the history of the country or area where his activities are concentrated. This applies also to research in Czechoslovakia. The following should help the researcher understand the people of Czechoslovakia and the evolution of their culture and customs.

The Western world is generally not aware of how ancient the Czech culture actually is nor how powerful and prosperous the kingdom of Bohemia was during the Middle Ages. The Czechs and Slovaks are among the most zealous members of the Slavic group of nations, yet they have deep spiritual and cultural connections with Western Europe. Bohemia, the westernmost province of present day Czechoslovakia, first appeared on the map of Europe during the period of Roman conquest. At that time the province was inhabited by a Celtic tribe, Boii, under the leadership of Boiohemus, from whom the province and its inhabitants received their names. Though the name Bohemia is utilized in America, it is not used in Czechoslovakia at all. The official title is Čechy, and the people call themselves Čechové (Czechs) and not Bohemians.

The Czech and Slovak branches of the Slavs appear in Čechy during the fifth century A.D., under the leadership of "praotec Čech" (forefather Czech), from whom the names of the area and the people are derived. For a number of centuries their descendants lived in a quasi-independent tribal organization, which developed into the Czech (Čechy), Moravian (Morava), Silesian (Slezsko), and Slovakian (Slovensko) provinces. In the seventh century these provinces were united with lower Austria and Poland, also inhabited by Slavic people, to form the Great Moravian Empire. The rulers of this empire persuaded two Greek monks, Cyril and Methodius, to bring Christianity to the population. They brought with them an alphabet, which they designed for the Slavic language and used for their translations of religious books and hymns into Slavic. They converted a large portion of the population to the Eastern form of Christianity. The Great Moravian Empire subsequently became an important Slavic center, from which both Christianity and Slavic culture spread to other nations of central and Eastern Europe.

5

In the early tenth century the Moravian Empire was invaded
by the Magyars, who in turn subjugated Slovakia. For the
next one thousand years the Czech and Slovak people, so
closely related by language, character, and manner of living, were separated. The fall of Slovakia at the beginning of the tenth century signaled the collapse of the
Moravian Empire. The seat of power then passed to Bohemia,
and the two Slavic peoples, Czechs and Moravians, merged
into one.

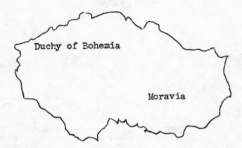

Duchy of Bohemia and Moravia (919-1125)

During this period, Bohemia was ruled by the strong, popular
dynasty of the Premyslides, who were titled princes and
dukes. One of the members of this dynasty was Prince Václav
(Wenceslas), who traveled widely in the interest of Christianity. In the twelfth century, Bohemia and Moravia
became members of the Holy Roman Empire--a large confedera-
tion of Christian states in central Europe. Though this
empire was ruled by German kings, all member countries enjoyed virtual independence. It was not until 1198 that the
České Země (Bohemia, Moravia, and Silesia) was elevated to
the status of a kingdom and the princes were granted the
title of king. They strongly immersed themselves in the
western culture and religion. As a result, the Greek Orthodox religion was replaced by Roman Catholicism.

The last king of the Premyslide dynasty died in 1306. After
a short interregnum, the rule of the České Země was taken
over by a king of the Luxemburg dynasty, which occurred as
a natural result of the marriage between King John of Luxemburg and the Czech Premyslide princess, Elizabeth. Their
son, Charles IV (1346-78) became the country's most popular ruler in history. His reign ushered in an era of unprecedented prosperity. In addition, he acquired the title of
emperor and thereby transferred the center of the Holy
Roman Empire to Prague.

King Charles's most significant contribution lies in the
elevation of the country's culture. In 1347 he founded the
University of Prague, now called the Charles University,

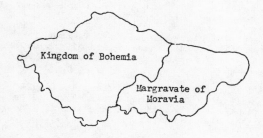

Kingdom of Bohemia and Margravate of Moravia (1378)

which at that time was the only institution of higher learning in central and eastern Europe. The University of Prague
also became the center of a new religious philosophy introduced by Jan Hus (1379-1415), a professor at the university
and a Catholic preacher in Betlemská chapel in Prague. He
found that many doctrines of the Catholic church, such as
the selling of indulgences and the limited participation of
the congregation in the Eucharist (only the priest partook
of both the bread and wine), departed from the norms established in the Bible. He consequently advocated that the
church return to the original teachings as outlined in the
Holy Scriptures. For his public statements, he was summoned
to the church council in Constance, Switzerland. Despite
the pass of safe conduct he had from the Holy Roman Emperor,
he was seized by papal forces, convicted of heresy without
the chance to defend himself, and finally burned at the
stake.

Although Jan Hus intended only to instigate corrections
within the Catholic church, his followers, under the leadership of Petr Chelčický (1390-1460), organized in 1457 their
own church in protest. This church was called Bratrská
Jednota (also known as the Moravian Brethren, Bohemian
Brethren, Unitas Fratrum, or the Church of United Brethren,
and, in Germany, Bruedergemeide or Herrnhutter). Although
the church was located in the center of staunch Roman and
Greek Catholic countries, it gained in popularity and in
time some 90 percent of the population of the České Země
was counted in its membership. The Holy Roman Empire waged
several crusades against the "Czech heretics," who at first
succeeded in defending themselves against great odds.

In spite of the limitations, the Bratrská Jednota continued
to pursue its cultural and literary goals. A committee,
under the leadership of Jan Blahoslav, prepared an excellent

translation of the Bible. This work was accomplished only after a lengthy study of the original languages of the Bible and through comparison with the Greek, Latin, and German texts. The result was published in 1579 in Kralice; hence the Czech title, "Kralická Bible." This translation, still used in the original, is a masterpiece of smooth, expressive language; and in some instances its accuracy exceeds that of the King James translation.

In 1618 the conflicts between the Catholics and Protestants in Europe resulted in the Thirty Years' War, devastating many areas in most of the European continent. The Hapsburgs, the Catholic Austrian dynasty, finally defeated the Czech insurgents in 1620 at the Battle of White Mountain (Bílá Hora), close to Prague. Many Czech leaders were executed and thousands of their followers exiled. Their estates and properties were confiscated and distributed among their tested, mainly German, royalists.

After the Battle of White Mountain, the members of the Bratrská Jednota were forced to practice their religion in secret. Religious persecution in Bohemia and Moravia became so severe that thousands were reduced to destitution or beggary. Many left their homes and crossed the borders into Saxony, Silesia, and Poland.

Foremost among the Bratrská Jednota exiles was Bishop Jan Komenský (John Comenius). He was, and still is, recognized as a "teacher of nations" for his efforts to modernize education. He wrote many volumes on the subject. Since as an exile he could not write in his native language, he wrote in Latin.

After the victory at White Mountain, the Hapsburgs launched an oppressive and cruel catholicization of the České Země. Governing from Vienna, they tried to mold the country into a province of their empire with a distinctly German character. The foreign owners of the treasured Czech estates held the population in a strict feudal system without relief until 1846.

In 1722 a small party of refugees, under the leadership of a carpenter, Christian David, reached Count Zinzendorf's estate in Saxony. He allowed them to settle on his estate and establish a village named Ochranov (Herrnhut), which later became the center for Protestant refugees from all over central Europe and a springboard for Moravian emigration to America.

The nineteenth century in the České Země as well as in Slovakia marks a cultural and nationalistic awakening. In both areas the people were extremely tired of foreign oppression. Prominent educated men began to prepare for a better future. This is the period of Czech and Slovak history that produced the most enlightened men, dedicated to the cause of their people. Language and grammar books, as well as language dictionaries, were published. The Austrian government had to make concessions to the demands of the Czech public; and, although the Czech language still was not elevated to the position of the official language, it was taught in schools and books were published in it. Other concessions of a more political nature were granted by the Hapsburgs; a desire for self-determination was strongly felt culminating at the end of World War I with the defeat of Austria and Germany. At that time the subjugated nations were set free.

In 1918 the Slovaks, free for the first time in over a millenium, together with the Czechs, formed the Czechoslovak Republic and the Slovak language became the secondary official language.

This very brief sketch of Czechoslovakian history describes primary events which are of importance in genealogical research. It should be read before a study is made of the chapters on "Sources for Genealogical Research in Czechoslovakia," "Language," Names," "Archives," and "Czech and Slovak Immigration to America."

BIBLIOGRAPHY

BIBLIOGRAFIE ČESKÉ HISTORIE. Prague, Historický klub [Historical club]: 1922. GL 943.7 A3c. In Czech.

    Bibliography of Czech historical works.

BIBLIOGRAFIE ČESKOSLOVENSKÉ HISTORIE. Prague: Československá akademie věd, 1955. GL 943.7 A3cs. In Czech.

    An enlargement, not a continuation of the preceding bibliography of Czechoslovakian history.

Bokeš, František. DEJINY SLOVENSKA A SLOVAKOV OD NAJSTAR-ŠEICH DOB PO OSLOBODENIE. Bratislava, 1946. In Slovak.

    The history of Slovakia and Slovaks from the earliest times to the era of liberation. A sound and judicious treatment of the history of the Slovak people under Magyar rule and later as part of the Republic.

Buresh, Vitus. HISTORICAL DOCUMENTS OF ANCIENT BOHEMIA. N.P., 1964. Part 1: microfilm 830,226. Part 2: microfilm 830,227.

    Part 1 is the life of St. Cyril and St. Methodius and a brief account of the baptisms in Moravia and Bohemia during the ninth and tenth centuries. Part 2 is the life of St. Ludmila, St. Václav, St. Procopius, and St. Vitus during the tenth-thirteenth centuries.

Českomoravské podniky tiskařské a vydavatelské. ČASOPIS PRO DĚJINY VENKOVA S PŘÍLOHOU SELSKÝ ARCHÍV. Prague, 1913.

Only 1 vol. available at the Genealogical Library, GL 943.7 B2d, or microfilm 908,258. In Czech.

> Periodical for history of rural Czechoslovakia. Since World War I and World War II, many old periodicals have been discontinued. This periodical can be valuable in finding information concerning past customs.

ČESKOSLOVENSKÁ VLASTIVĚDA. 10 vols. Prague, 1929-36. In Czech.

> Covers the main areas of the nation's life, that is, art, literature, the state, geography, music, and so forth. Volume 4 and the supplement cover history. Extensive bibliography.

Horecky, Pal. I., ed. EAST CENTRAL EUROPE. Chicago: University of Chicago, 1969. GL 940 A3h.

> A guide to basic histories.

Hosák, Ladislav. DĚJINY MORAVSKÉHO SLOVENSKA. Břeclav, Moravia, 1927. In Czech.

> History of the Moravian part of Slovakia. Part 3 concerns religious and cultural conditions before 1620.

Husa, Václav. NAŠE NÁRODNÍ MINULOST V DOKUMENTECH. Prague, 1954. In Czech.

> Selected documents, in Czech but with Slovak translation. Illustrates Czech and Slovak history up to 1785 with emphasis on documents showing class conflicts. Very scholarly collection, however, only marginally helpful for the study of genealogy.

Janoušek, B., ed. JIHOČESKÝ SBORNÍK HISTORICKÝ. 29 vols. České Budějovice, Bohemia: Krajské vlastivědné museum (Regional historical and ethnographical museum), 1928-60. In Czech.

> Articles on South Bohemian history, mainly from the Hussite period and after. Contains indexes organized by author, classified subject, biography, and geography.

Jelinek, Bretislav. DIE BOEHMEN IN KAMPFE UM IHRE SELB-STAENDIGKEIT, 1618-48. [Bohemians in the contest for independence]. Prague, 1916. GL microfilm 24390. In German.

> Includes a biography of each of the combatants in the Thirty Years' War.

Jesina, Cestmir. THE BIRTH OF CZECHOSLOVAKIA. Washington, D.C.: Czechoslovak National Council of America, 1968. GL 943.7 H4c.

A collection of documents illuminating the formation of the Czechoslovak Republic in 1918.

K POCIATKOM MAD'ARIZACIE [The beginning of the Magyarization of Slovaks]. Bratislava, 1927. In Slovak.

This focuses on the language question under Maria Theresia and Joseph II, 1740-90. Good bibliography.

Kaminsky, Howard. A HISTORY OF THE HUSSITE REVOLUTION. Berkeley and Los Angeles: University of California Press, 1967. GL 943.71 K2k.

Kerner, Robert J. BOHEMIA IN THE EIGHTEENTH CENTURY. New York: n.p., 1932.

This focuses on the reigns of Joseph II and Leopold II, and is based on study of Vienna Archives.

Krofta, Kamil. A SHORT HISTORY OF CZECHOSLOVAKIA. New York: Robert McBride, 1934.

A good, highly condensed survey of Czech and Slovak history to about 1930; it is essentially factual, sound and unbiased, following strict chronological lines.

Mašek, Josef. TÁBOR V HUSITSKÉM REVOLUČNÍM HNUTÍ [Tábor in the Hussite revolutionary movement]. 2 vols. Prague, 1952-56. In Czech.

Detailed study of the relations of Tábor, the Hussite capital, with the rest of Bohemia. Many helpful maps and tables.

Oddo, Gilbert Lawrence. SLOVAKIA AND ITS PEOPLE. New York: Robert Speller and Sons, 1960. GL 943.7 H2o.

Concise analysis of Slovakia's past and present.

Odložilík, Otakar. THE CAROLINE UNIVERSITY, 1348-1948. Prague, 1948.

Best short summary of the history of the oldest university east of Rhine: the Charles University of Prague, also known as Caroline University.

OD PRAVĚKU K DNESKU [From prehistoric times to today]. 2 vols. Prague: Historický klub, 1930. GL 943.7 H2p. In Czech.

OTTŮV SLOVNÍK NAUČNÝ. 28 vols. Prague: 1888-1909. GL Ref 030.437 Ot8e or microfilm 873,864 to 873,891. In Czech.

Standard Czech encyclopedia, richly illustrated. It contains helpful maps and plans.

OTTŮV SLOVNÍK NAUČNÝ NOVÉ DOBY. 6 vols. Prague, 1930-43.
In Czech.

A supplement to the preceding item.

Palacký, Frantisek. DĚJINY NÁRODU ČESKÉHO V ČECHÁCH A NA
MORAVĚ. 1843. Reprint. Prague: B. Koči, 1907. GL 943.7
H2pa or GL microfilm 446,642. In Czech.

History of the Czech nation in Bohemia and Moravia.
Considered to be the most scholarly work on the
subject.

Placht, Otto. LIDNATOST A SPOLEČENSKÁ SKLADBA ČESKÉHO STÁTU
V 16.-18.STOLETÍ. Prague: Československá akademie věd a
umění, 1957. GL 943.7 H6p. In Czech.

Population density and social structure of the Czech
state in the sixteenth to eighteenth centuries.

Rechcigl, Miloslav. THE CZECHOSLOVAK CONTRIBUTION TO
WORLD CULTURE. The Hague: Mouton, 1964. GL Ref. 943.7 H2r.

An evaluation of the contribution of many Czechoslovak
individuals in various fields of endeavor.

Roubík, Frantisek. PŘÍRUČKA VIASTIVEDNÉ PRACE. Vol. 4. Know-
your-country series. Prague: Spolecnost přátel starožit-
nosti [Society of Friends of Antiquities], 1947. GL 943.7
B3k. In Czech.

Concerned primarily with history and geography.

Schwartz, Michael. DIE SLOVAKEI, DIE JUENGSTE STAAT EUROPAS.
Leipzig, Germany: W. Goldman, 1939. GL 943.73 H2s. In
German.

Offers an outsider's point of view regarding Slovakia.

Seton-Watson, Robert William. A HISTORY OF CZECHS AND
SLOVAKS. 1943. Reprint. Hamden, Conn.: 1965. GL 943.7
H2s.

An excellent account of the changing structure of the
lands of the Bohemian crown; however, it tends to
view Bohemia from the Austrian point of view.

SOUPIS PRAMENŮ K DĚJINÁM FEUDÁLNÍHO ÚTISKU, 16TH-19TH CEN-
TURY. Prague: Československá akademie věd a umění, 1954.
GL 943.7 H2r. In Czech.

An inventory of sources for the history of feudal
oppression from the sixteenth through the nineteenth
centuries.

Strakhovsky, Leonid Ivanovich. A HANDBOOK OF SLAVIC
STUDIES. Cambridge, Mass.: Harvard University Press,
1949. GL Ref 940 H2Ls.

> A well-presented description of the history, geog-
> raphy, and political conditions in all Slavic lands.

Sturm, Rudolf. CZECHOSLOVAKIA, A BIBLIOGRAPHICAL GUIDE.
Bibliographic Guides Series. Washington D.C.: Library of
Congress, 1967. LCCN 68-60019.

Tobolka, Zdeněk. POLITICKÉ DĚJINY ČESKOSLOVENSKÉHO NÁRODA,
1932-37. 5 vols. N.p., n.d. In Czech.

> A political history of the Czechoslovak nation.

Uhlíř, František. TĚŠÍNSKÉ SLEZSKO. Prague, 1946. In
Czech.

> A detailed history and demographic study of the
> region Teschen-Silesia.

Sources Concerning the German Minority in Czechoslovakia

Dobiáš, Josef. NĚMECKÉ OSÍDLENÍ OSTRŮVKU JIHLAVSKÉHO.
Prague: Státní archívní škola, 1931. GL 943.723 F2d. In
Czech.

> A record of German immigration to Iglau district of
> Moravia. Valuable for genealogy.

Franzel, Emil. SUDETENDEUTSCHE GESCHICHTE; EINE VOLKSTUEM-
LICHE DARSTELLUNG. Augsburg: A. Kraft, 1958. GL 943.7
F2gf. In German.

> A history of Sudeten Germans in Czechoslovakia from
> the German point of view.

Frinta, Antonin. ŽITAVSKO V ČESKÝCH DĚJINÁCH. Prague:
Orbis, 1947. GL 943.212/Z H2f. In Czech.

> Zittau district in Czech history. Good genealogical
> source.

Hanika, Josef. SIEDLUNGSGESCHICHTE UND LAUTGEOGRAPHIE DES
DEUTSCHEN HAULANDES IN DER MITTELSLOWAKEI. Munich: R.
Lerche, 1952. GL 943.7 H2h. In German.

> The history of German settlers in central Slovakia.
> Important for genealogical study.

Luza, Radomir. THE TRANSFER OF SUDETEN GERMANS. New York:
University Press, 1964. GL 943.7 H2L.

> A study of Czech-German relations from 1933-62.

Wiskeman, Elizabeth. CZECHS AND GERMANS. London: Macmillan and Co., 1967. GL 943.7 H4w.

A study of the struggle between Czechs and Germans in the historic provinces of Bohemia and Moravia.

Chapter 3
GEOGRAPHY

From the signing of the Versailles Treaty in 1918 until 1949, Czechoslovakia was composed of the following provinces: Bohemia (Čechy), Moravia (Morava), Silesia (Slezsko), and Slovakia (Slovensko). Lower Carpathia or Ruthenia (Podkarpatská Rus) was also included until 1945, when it became part of the Soviet Union. This organization of provinces simply continued the administrative structure which existed prior to 1918. In 1949 this provincial division was eliminated and administrative districts (oblasti) were established. Both the provinces and the districts were further subdivided into counties (okresy). Additional information on this will be included in the chapter dealing with archives. For our purposes, the term České Země (Czech Lands) refers only to the three original provinces of Czechoslovakia: Bohemia, Moravia, and Silesia.

From the time of the Roman Empire down to the present, the western and southern borders of the České Země have remained unchanged. These borders remained uniform whether the area of the České Země was called the Duchy of Bohemia and Moravia or the Kingdom of Bohemia or whether it was under the domination of Austria or later a free Czechoslovakia. This uniformity arises primarily from the fact that the western border of Čechy is formed by high mountains with very few passes. In the eastern province of Silesia, however, where no such natural boundaries exist, the borders were in a continuous state of flux. Slovakia is not shown on maps of Czechoslovakia prior to 1918 since it was then under the domination of the Hungarian Empire.

The Versailles Treaty restored to this group of small historic states the right of self-determination and self-government. These rights had been lost in Slovakia some thousand years previously and in Bohemia and Moravia in 1620. For the following 300 years the Czechs and Moravians were dominated by the Hapsburgs and involuntarily functioned as a part of the Austrian Empire.

With the foregoing as a short introduction to Czech geography, it is possible to understand how geography can affect genealogical research. It should be noted that despite the changes of government throughout the history of Czechoslovakia, the records of the people have always remained in the locality where they originated.

The Hapsburg domination of Czechoslovakia explains why so many immigrants coming to the United States from Czechoslovakia before 1918 were identified not as Czechs, but as Austrians, and why so many old records and documents list the capital of Czechoslovakia, Prague, as a city in Austria. Present-day Czechoslovakia is a long, narrow country which borders the Soviet Union on the east, Hungary on the south and southeast, Austria on the south and southwest, Germany on the west and northwest, and Poland on the north. To the citizens who lived along these boundaries, the borders themselves were not inviolate. People married across them and were allowed to settle in the country of their spouses. Thus, one can find many Polish names recorded in the parishes of Czechoslovakia and vice versa. As a rule, people did not roam far from home in search of a spouse. A German, for example, who married a Czech girl, more than likely resided in a village close to the border. If the church records where he settled do not indicate his origin, it is advisable to study a good, detailed map of the area and then search the records of the adjacent communities for the elusive foreign ancestor.

The capital of both Čechy and the Republic as a whole is Prague (Praha). The capital of Moravia is Brno. Opava is the capital city of Slezsko, while Bratislava is the capital of Slovensko. Although the official language of the country is Czech, Slovak is spoken in Slovensko. Czech and Slovak differ sufficiently that native speakers of each often have difficulty understanding one another. Foreign languages are taught in grade school and continue throughout one's formal education. Consequently, many Czech citizens speak, in addition to their mother tongue, French, Russian, German, and English. This linguistic dexterity is born of necessity. Czechoslovakia is situated in the center of Europe and is a hub of international activity for commerce, education, art, music, and science.

No research should be undertaken in Czechoslovakia until the ancestral residence has been unmistakably located. The Genealogical Library has an excellent postal guide (ADMINISTRATIVE LEXIKON DER CZECHOSLOVAKISCHEN REPUBLIK, GL 943.7 E5a), which gives the name of each locality where a post office is located, the religious denominations for which there is a parish, and the name of the county where it is situated. There are also good maps (see bibliography following this chapter), which help define the location of the county, and thus the family residence. This is of extreme importance, since the same name of the locality could appear in various parts of the county. For example, in the Gemeindelexikon there are 112 places with the name of Nová Ves. One can find sixty places bearing the name Lhota. Many of these names are preceded by an adjective, such as Malá (Small) Lhota. There are families here in the United States who know only that their ancestor came from Malá Lhota. To search the records of all the Malá Lhotas in Czechoslovakia would be, if not impossible, very frustrating. One must try to identify the place from other information. The chapter on research in America gives some helpful suggestions which could bring results.

The Gemeindelexikon, as well as the majority of other aids used for research in Czechoslovakia, is very well indexed. In order to use them, however, one must know something about the Czech alphabet. Although the alphabet is given on pages 122-23, some rules are repeated here to emphasize their importance. In alphabetizing, all words starting with a consonant above which there is a háček (check mark) follow those words which have no such mark. For example, Říp follows Rymavská Sobota; Znojmo precedes Žakovice; Sušice before Stěpánov. The same rule about the háček applies to consonants which appear later in the word, the consonants without a háček appear before those with a háček. For example, it is Nespeky before Nešov, Evan before Evaň. In a great majority of cases the háček above Czech names has disappeared in America, making it more difficult to determine the locale of the ancestral origin. If such an alteration is suspected, one should check the index under the consonant both with and without a háček.

"Ch" is considered one sound and follows the letter "h": Hradec-Chomutov. It is pronounced as in the word "loch." The diacritic, which appears above some vowels as in the word "čárka" does not place the word in a separate alphabetical order.

As already indicated, many Czech place names consist of two words, an adjective and a noun. As a rule, the indexes list the locality under both, for example, Mladá Boleslav - Boleslav Mladá.

Many cities and villages in Czechoslovakia are officially named as being "above" a certain river or lake, for example, Týn nad Vltavou, (Tyn above Vltava). This is sometimes written Týn n/Vlt. If everything else fails in determining the county of the origin of the family, this might be of help. In preparing ancestral records, it is important to list the complete name of the place, even though at times it may be a nuisance. The names of places and individuals should never be abbreviated in genealogical work.

At the present time in Czechoslovakia there are some 15 million people living in an area of 49,354 square miles. In the past, the population was primarily rural. However, at present only 38 percent of the population is engaged in agriculture. Many Czechs work in iron and steel mills or other industries that produce machinery, glass, china, textiles, processed foods, chemicals, boots and shoes, gloves, lumber, and paper.

Traditionally, it has not been easy to become a master shoemaker, lumberman, or even a farmer. A young man had to serve an apprenticeship for a period of four years before he was

allowed to open his own shop, or even hire out as an assistant. If he decided to emigrate to America, he generally
practiced his trade or profession in his new home. This
tendency can be of great help in locating your ancestor's
point of origin. It is doubtful that an American farmer
would have come from Prague or any other large city. However, this is not a hard-and-fast rule. A city boy had
no chance to learn farming; on the other hand, the child
of a farmer could learn a trade, profession or skill, if
all members of the farmer's family were willing to make a
tremendous sacrifice. My father, for example, was born
and raised on a small, poor farm. Since he was unusually
gifted with a thirst for knowledge, musical talent, and a
rich baritone voice, all his teachers urged him to go to
the nearby city and work for a better education. While he
was gone, his brother and sister had to accomplish his work
load on the farm. When he completed the Teachers' Institute he obtained a position as a teacher in a school near
Prague. He enrolled in the Musical Academy in Prague; but,
in order to attend, he had to walk there and back daily--
there was no money for train fare. If he had ever emigrated
to America and given his birthplace as a small village, a
future researcher would not look for his marriage and us,
his children, in Prague.

All good encyclopedias have sections dealing with Czechoslovakia, its school system, economy, country life, history,
geography, and so forth. The genealogical researcher should
read them carefully. They can help him to localize the
search for his ancestors. The research will indicate that
there have been plenty of farmers; though half of the soil
of the Republic can presently be farmed, this percentage
was much higher in the past. Western Bohemia, Southern
Moravia, and Slovakia have deposits of coal. Throughout the
country there also are rich veins of silver and gold.
Northeastern Moravia contains iron ore and Northeast Bohemia has some uranium mines. All this combined with the
knowledge of the family background can help narrow down the
locale of the ancestral origin. The climate is much like
that of southern Canada, with hot summers and cold winters.

The most important schools of higher learning are Charles
University, founded in Prague in 1348; František Palacký
University, founded in Olomouc in 1576; Czech Technical
University, first founded in Prague in 1907; Masaryk University, founded in Brno in 1919; and Slovak University of
Bratislava, founded in 1919. At the present time there are
almost 50,000 students enrolled in Charles University and
its branches, with a comparable number of students attending other universities.

Since Czechoslovak people are basically pious and God-fear-
ing, religion is still a very important factor in their
lives. The present-day regime, however, puts the value of
the common good--the state--above religion or the individual. Churches must conduct their activities accordingly.

About three fourths of the population still belong to the Roman Catholic Church; almost 1 million individuals are Protestants; an equal number belong to the Czechoslovak Church; some 50,000 are members of the Eastern Orthodox Church; and about 50,000 are Jews. The records of these churches are discussed in the chapter on "Sources for Genealogical Research in Czechoslovakia."

Traditional Czechoslovakian handicrafts can play a role in identifying family origins. For special occasions the people in small villages still wear the local costumes, rich with colorful embroidery and handmade laces. There are many costume styles, each associated with a particular area. The area of the ancestral home can often be determined by the style of costume worn by the people. Likewise, other decorative arts can be used to pinpoint a locale. People decorate their farmhouses, gates or fences with handpaintings of colorful patterns. Pottery and the handweaving of wool or flax are two other decorative folk arts which can be used to help trace a particular town or village.

The monetary unit is the koruna (crown), abbreviated as Kčs, consisting of 100 halér. Since the value of money fluctuates on the international market, it is difficult to state here the exchange value of the koruna in U.S. dollars. In 1975 you could exchange one U.S. dollar for 5.10 Kčs, with a generous extra allowance to entice the tourists.

What are the typical Czechs and Slovaks like? It is difficult for the author, who was born and educated in Czechoslovakia, not to be prejudiced. However, I shall try to be objective. Czechs are of average height and slender, with fewer cases of obesity in later stages of their lives than other nationalities. Color of hair is normally light brown; there is no predominent eye color among them. The Czechs are anything but mentally and physically lazy. They like order and organization in both their work and leisure. Sports and outdoor activities are very popular. The Czechs excel in skiing, swimming, hockey, tennis, soccer, and dancing. They love their families, are loyal and proud, but at the same time are foxy enough to bow to temporarily insoluble situations. As a rule they are of sunny dispositions and love to laugh, often at themselves--but don't make the mistake of laughing at them! They are hospitable and love to socialize. A visitor finds them delightful and easy to get along with. Other than the foregoing, they are excessively critical, ornerier than the proverbial Swedes, quarrelsome, and at times tight-fisted. They get along better with their foreign neighbors than with their own kind. However, when personal or national emergencies arrive they feel and act as one.

BIBLIOGRAPHY

ADMINISTRATIVE GEMEINDELEXIKON DER CZECHOSLOVAKISCHEN REPUBLIK. 2 vols. Prague: Státní úřad statisticky, 1927-28.

GL 943.7 E5a and microfilm 496,719 (1st vol.), 496,720 (2d vol.) Mostly in German.

Administrative gazeteer of the Czechoslovak republic. The judicial and political divisions have been changed, and so this lexicon has been replaced by more recent issues. There are several helpful features. In addition to Bohemia, Moravia, Silesia, and Slovakia, the volumes also contain Karpathorussland, which was added to Russia after World War II. The addition at the end of each of the volumes contains German, Polish, Russian, and Hungarian versions of the names of the localities. Since the text places each locality in a certain county, listing also the larger political unit to which the locality might have belonged, the use of the two volumes is still recommended.

ATLAS ČESKOSLOVENSKÉ REPUBLIKY. Prague, 1935. In Czech.

In view of the territorial changes after World War II and the political changes of the Socialist regime, it is now obsolete.

ATLAS DE LA REPUBLIQUE TCHECOSLOVAQUIE. Prague: Orbis, n.d. In French.

AUTOATLAS ČESKOSLOVENSKA. Bratislava: Slovenská kartografia, 1971. GL Ref. 943.7 E3as. In Czech. Scale 1:400.000

Brandrupp, A. .BOEHMEN, MAEHREN UND OESTERREICHISCH SCHLESIEN. 1898. GL Map 943.7 E7p. In German. Scale 1:2,000.000.

Map of Bohemia, Moravia, and Austrian Silesia.

Černý, František and Vasa, Pavel. MORAVSKÉ JMÉNA MÍSTNÍ. Brno: Matice Moravská, 1927. In Czech.

A scholarly work tracing the origins of the names of Moravian localities.

ČESKOSLOVENSKO. Poznáváme Svět (series). Prague: Kartografické nakladatelství, 1967. GL 943.7 E7c. In Czech.

Part of the series "We Learn to Know the World."

ČESKOSLOVENSKO V MAPÁCH. Prague, 1954. In Czech.

Various sections of Czechoslovakia presented in maps showing physical characteristics, economic and industrial situations as well as minority settlements.

Doskočil, Karel. POPIS ČECH R.1654 [Description of Bohemia in 1654]. Berní Rula. 2 vols. Prague: Státní pedagogické nakladatelství, 1953. GL 943.7 B4b. In Czech.

(See chapter 5, "Sources for Genealogical Research in Czechoslovakia," and section on tax records, p. 53.)

Great Britain. Army Map Service. Corps of Engineers. London: War Office and Air Ministry, 1956. Colored map. GL Map 940 E7gb. Scale 1:1,000.000.

Covers most of Czechoslovakia and parts of neighboring Austria, Germany, Poland, and Hungary.

HISTORICAL MAP OF MORAVIA. N.p., n.d. GL Map 943.7 E7mor. In Czech. Scale not known.

Historical map of Moravia.

Homann, Johann Baptiste. REGNI BOHEMIA. Nuernberg, n.d. GL E.S.Q. 940 E7c, No. 17, (in Latin), or GL microfilm 599,738.

The Kingdom of Bohemia, Duchy of Silesia, Moravia, and East German areas.

Hosák, Ladislav. MÍSTNÍ JMÉNA NA MORAVĚ A VE SLEZSKU. Prague: Československá akademie věd, n.d. GL 943.7 E2h, Vol. 1. A-L. In Czech.

Place names in Moravia and Silesia, their origin and subsequent changes.

Huhn, Eugen. TOPOGRAPHISCH-STATISTISCH-HISTORISCHES LEXIKON VON DEUTSCHLAND. Berlin: Bibliographisches Institut, 1846. GL microfilms 491,132 (Hb-Laz), 491,111 (Lb-Oz), others not available at GL. In German.

Topographical, statistical, and historical lexikon of Germany--also includes Bohemia.

Kredel, Otto, comp. DEUTSCH-FREMDSPRACHIGES ORTSNAMENVERZEICHNIS. Berlin: Deutsche Verlagsgesellschaft, 1931. GL Q 940 E5kt, 4 parts. Czechoslovakia is in part 3. In German.

A list of localities in Europe by countries, for which there is a German name.

Kuchař, Karel. EARLY MAPS OF BOHEMIA, MORAVIA AND SILESIA. Prague: Ústřední správa geodezie a kartografie, 1961. GL Q 943.7 E3b. Summaries in French and German.

MAPA KULTURNÍCH PAMÁTEK ČESKOSLOVENSKA. Prague: Kartografie, 1972. GL 943.7 E3m. In Czech.

A map showing the locations of cultural and historical monuments of the past.

Meynen, R. SUDETENDEUTSCHER ATLAS. Muenchen: Arbeitsgemeinschaft zur Wahrung Sudetendeutscher Interesses, 1954. GL Q 943.7 E7m. In German.

Atlas of the Sudeten German region.

MORAVIA. N.p. n.d. GL E.S. Map 943.7 E7mor. In Czech.
Scale not known.

Historical map of Moravia.

Mueller, Johann Christoph. MAPPA GEOGRAPHICA REGNI BOHEMIAE
AND CONSPECTUS GENERALIS REGNI BOHEMIAE. Prague: Geogra-
ficky ustav Karlovy university, 1934. In Latin.

Historical map showing Bohemia in 1720.

Pfohl, Ernst. ORIENTIERUNG-LEXIKON DER TSCHECHOSLOVAKISCHEN
REPUBLIK. Liberec, Bohemia: Gebrueder Stiepel, 1931. Xerox
copy of the original. GL Q 943.7 E5p, or microfilm 583,456.
In German.

Gazeteer of Czechoslovakia, 1931.

PLZEN-AUTOMAPA. Prague: Kartograficke nakladatelstvi,
1967. GL Map 943,712 E7p. In Czech. Scale 1:200,000

Road map of the Pilsen region, Bohemia.

POLAND AND CZECHOSLOVAKIA. Washington, D.C.: The National
Geographic Society, 1958. GL E.S.Q. Map 940 E7pc. Scale:
1:2,154,240.

Profous, Antonin. MISTNI JMENA V CECHACH, JEJICH VZNIK,
PUVODNI VYZNAM A ZMENY. 4 vols. Prague: Nakladatelstvi
ceskoslovenske akademie ved, 1954-60. GL Ref 943.7 A2p.
In Czech.

Place names in Czechoslovakia, their sources, original meaning, and later changes.

Roubik, Frantisek. SOUPIS A MAPA ZANIKLYCH OSAD V CECHACH.
Prague: ceskoslovenska akademie ved, 1959. GL Ref 943.7
E5z. In Czech.

A list and a map of localities in Bohemia which are
no longer in existence.

Schwarz, Ernst. DIE ORTSNAMEN DER SUDETENLAENDER ALS GES-
CHICHTSQUELLE. Vol. 1. Handbuch der Sudetendeutschen Kul-
tursgeschichte. Munich: R. Larche, 1961. In German.

Place names in the Sudeten region as historical
sources.

Semik, M. CESKOSLOVENSKA REPUBLIKA. Prague: Neubert a Syn-
ove, 1936. GL Map 943.7 E7a. In Czech. Scale 1:500,000.

A collection of 3 detailed maps: (1) East Czechoslovakia, (2) Middle Czechoslovakia, and (3) West Czechoslovakia.

SHORT GAZETEER OF CZECHOSLOVAKIA. London: Permanent Committee on Geographical Names for British Official Use, 1958. GL Q 943.7 E5po.

STATISTICKÝ LEXIKON OBCÍ V ČESKOSLOVENSKÉ REPUBLICE. Vol. 2. Prague: n.p., 1924. GL 943.7 E5s. In Czech.

Only volume 2 available at the GL--MORAVA and SLEZSKO. Statistical lexikon of places in Moravia and Silesia where there are post offices.

Sulimierski, Filip. SLOVNÍK GEOGRAFICZNÝ KROLESTWA POLSKIEGO I INNÝCH KRAJUV SLOVANSKÝCH. Warsaw, 1880-1902. Vols. 1-15, in alphabetical order on microfilm at GL. In Polish.

Geographical dictionary of the Polish kingdom and other Slavic countries, including Czechoslovakia.

TOPOGRAFICKO STATISTICKÝ SLOVNÍK ČECH. N.p., 1870. GL Staff 943.71 E5t. In Czech.

Topographical statistical dictionary of Bohemia.

Chapter 4
CZECH AND SLOVAK IMMIGRATION TO AMERICA

Before research is conducted in Czechoslovakia itself, all appropriate genealogical sources in America should be thoroughly examined. Only after the name of the original immigrant from Czechoslovakia, as well as his date and place of birth, have been unmistakably established, should foreign research be initiated. It is important then to be aware of the history of Bohemian immigration, the particular problems that arose, and of some of the pertinent sources and statistics.

One recurring problem in tracing Czech ancestry should be mentioned at the outset. In the chapter on "Geography," it has been stated that many of the immigrants arriving from Czechoslovakia between 1620 and 1918 were mistakenly labeled as Austrians since their native country during these 3 centuries was under Austrian domination. In the American immigration records it is difficult to separate those who were born in Bohemia from those who, although their names were Czech, were born in Austria proper. Statistics are reliable only if they specify that the immigrant came from Bohemia. Probably many Bohemian arrivals were enumerated in the statistics concerning Austria.

The first known Czech immigrant to come to America was Augustin Herman (also known as Augustine Herrman, Bohemian), a religious refugee from Bohemia, who came to New Amsterdam (New York) in 1633. In 1660-61 he resided in Maryland, where he founded the Bohemian Manor. He was a surveyor by profession and among his greatest contributions to his new country was the drawing of an accurate map of Virginia and Maryland. The map is entitled "Virginia and Maryland As It is Planted and Inhabited This Present Year 1670 Surveyed and Exactly Drawn by the Labour and Endeavour of Augustine Herrman, Bohemiensis." Herman also has the distinction of being the first foreigner ever naturalized in America (1673).

Another settler of distinction was Frederick Philipse. As this version of his name suggests, he was one of the Czech exiles after 1620 who found his first home abroad in Holland. Then, together with other Dutch Protestant refugees, he migrated to America. The Manor Hall in Yonkers, New York, which Philipse built in 1682, is one of the finest specimens

of extant local Dutch architecture. Philipse also erected
a church at Tarrytown, believed to be the oldest extant
church building in New York State. He became a very successful merchant and was referred to as the "Bohemian Merchant Prince." Before the Philipses arrived in America,
they took part in the unsuccessful rebellion against the
Austrian king. In the land of their adoption 155 years
later, their descendants joined the king's cause in the War
of Independence, but again lost. Their huge estate in
Westchester County, New York, comprising 156,000 acres, was
seized and, in 1785, sold at auction by the state of New
York. Utterly ruined, they left America, together with
other royalists, for England. In the volumes listed in the
bibliography, there might be clues and data concerning the
ancestral locale of the Philipse family on Bohemia, and
also some information concerning their descendants who remained in America.

Many of the Czechs who came to this country in the eighteenth century were members of the Moravian church and came
as religious and political exiles from Bohemia and Moravia.
They took refuge first in the countries neighboring Bohemia.
One group following the teachings of John Hus settled in
Ochranov (Herrnhut, Saxony) and succeeded in converting
some Germans to their faith. Together with their German
converts, they later emigrated to America. As early as
1735 a Moravian colony was established in Savannah, Georgia,
where John Wesley, the founder of Methodism in England, was
present at the ordination of the first Czech pastor, Anthony
Seifert. In 1741 the Moravians founded the city of Bethlehem, Pennsylvania, which later became the religious and
cultural center of their activities. In 1752 a group of
their adherents went to North Carolina and established the
city of Salem, which is now the headquarters of their work
in the South. With the exception of their travels for mis-
sionary work among the Indians, for many years the Moravians
remained near the East Coast.

At the insistence of their patron, Count Zinzendorf of
Herrnhut, the Moravians kept excellent records of their
congregations. The church registers, along with several
other valuable genealogical sources, were usually kept in
a chest or closet in the parish itself. Later they were
collected and placed in central archives in Bethlehem,
Pennsylvania and Winston-Salem, North Carolina. Another
valuable source of information concerning individual members of this Moravian church is the series of TRANSACTIONS
OF THE MORAVIAN HISTORICAL SOCIETY (Moravian Historical Society, Whitefield House, Nazareth, Pennsylvania). For the
researchers of Czech-Moravian ancestry, the most important
is volume 9 which contains a list of the Czech and Moravian
immigrants to Saxony. Unless the church registers or the
TRANSACTIONS yield some clues, it is almost impossible to
identify and trace the place of the origin of this particular group of immigrants. The difficulty is compounded by
the fact that their names may have been germanized or angli-

cized beyond recognition or simply translated into English.

From about 1650 to the beginning of the nineteenth century, few residents of the Czech lands were able to emigrate to America, and then only illegally. At the beginning of the nineteenth century, a small trickle of Czech immigrants to America began. Several of those who came were highly educated. One of these newcomers was Dr. Antonin Dignovity, a physician, linguist, well-known explorer and inventor, and a personal friend of Sam Houston. Another was Jan Nepomucen Neumann, bishop of Philadelphia, who is considered the founder of the American church school system.

By the 1840s the trickle had become a veritable stream. The political upheavals of 1848 (after which the Hapsburg authorities gave the Czechs the right to emigrate) and the economic oppression of the Czech peasants by the Austrian nobility brought thousands of Czech immigrants to this country. In the 1850s the number of Czechs in America reached 20,000, which does not include the descendants of those who came between 1620-1840. According to the statistical reports based on U.S. census returns, in 1870 there were 40,289 new Czech immigrants in this country. There can be little doubt that many of the 30,508 persons listed as Austrians were also of Czech parentage.

The majority of Czech immigrants from 1850 to 1880 went to Texas and the Midwest. The Czech farmer immigrants settled in Nebraska, Iowa, Wisconsin, Minnesota, and Texas. Those who located in the cities concentrated in New York, Cleveland, Chicago, Milwaukee, St. Louis, Cedar Rapids, and Omaha. The first Czech Catholic parish was organized in 1854 in St. Louis and the first Czech Protestant church in 1867 in Ely, Iowa.

The Slovakian immigrants who came to this country en masse after 1880 were largely unskilled workers and found employment in the mines, factories, and steel mills of Pennsylvania, New York, New Jersey, and Ohio. The largest Slovakian settlement in the United States is in Pittsburgh, Pennsylvania. The military also provided employment. A number of Czech volunteers joined the Union Army during the Civil War. Many of these were Slovakian, resulting in an attempt to form a special Bohemian-Slavic battalion.

With this preliminary information, we can now concentrate on the analysis of individual research problems and suggest some sources where one can search for clues to ancestral origins in Czechoslovakia.

The reasons for emigration before the 1800s were mostly political and religious. Many Czechs left their homes in bitterness and were eager to take a productive part in their new country. They translated their names or changed them so that their new neighbors could pronounce them. (See chapter on "Names.") As mentioned earlier in this chapter, no one kept records of these refugees with the exception of the Moravians. These immigrants did not settle in one place for any length of time but were forever pushing ahead in search of religious liberty and peace. Even if these early settlers were listed in any of the preserved passenger lists and their names had not yet been changed, there would be no information concerning their ancestral home in the Czech lands. All this makes it almost impossible to trace them back to their mother country.

The Czech immigrants who came to America from 1800 to 1500 were motivated by economic considerations. They belonged largely to the working classes or were farmers. The land in America, particularly unsettled territory west of Ohio, did not have to be purchased. Under the Homestead Act, it was given to anyone who was willing to work it and, within the prescribed length of time, develop it by building some structures for human and animal habitation. The soil was rich and productive, but it was necessary to clear it of all wild growth (trees, matted shrubs) and rocks. There was no time or money for frills. Difficulties with the Indians, who resented these intruders, also had to be dealt with. Many families of the first Czech settlers were completely annihilated. Many, however, persevered, writing to friends and relatives in Czechoslovakia and telling them that they owned their own land. This served as a strong enticement to their relatives, neighbors, and friends still in Czechoslovakia to also emigrate and join them in the new locality. Based on this practice, one can assume that the majority of Bohemian settlers in one area in America was also from the same locale in Bohemia. If all else fails in locating the ancestral home, this is something to be mindful of. Otherwise, there are but few sources one can turn to for information concerning these immigrants.

The U.S. government kept lists of passengers arriving on the eastern seaboard from 1820 on. These lists were later deposited in the National Archives. Microfilm copies of these can be obtained from the Genealogical Society. The following are available through the services of the Latter-Day Saints Branch libraries:

PORT	CUSTOM PASSENGER LISTS	INDEXES
Baltimore	1820-91	1820-1952
Boston	1820-74	1848-91
New Orleans	1820-1902	1853-1952
New York	1820-97	1820-46
Philadelphia	1800-1882	1800-1948
Certain minor ports	1820-73	

To make a search of the passenger lists, one has to know the date of the arrival and the port through which the immigrants were admitted. Unfortunately, not all the indexes are complete and available for all time periods. The passenger lists give the names of the immigrants, their ages and only the country from which they came. This limits the information concerning the original Czech, Moravian, and Slovak immigrants merely to Austria. If one succeeds in locating the immigrant family in the passenger lists, genealogically the most important data he finds is the date of their arrival and also the names of various members of the family and others who may have come with them.

The emigrants from Germany and the former Austrian Empire used the German ports of Bremen and Hamburg to embark for countries overseas. Though the passenger lists for the port of Bremen were destroyed during World War II, the Hamburg immigration lists have been preserved. The Hamburg lists contain records from 1837 to the present and are deposited in the Hamburg State Archives. The Genealogical Library of the Latter-Day Saints Church has microfilmed lists covering the period 1850-1934 and indexes including the years 1855-1934. They are more complete than the lists kept by the captains of American vessels and in many instances contain the exact place of origin of the immigrant family. I am not listing the call numbers of these microfilms because of the great number of reels of film. I suggest that the interested researcher work through the Latter-Day Saints branch library closest to him. Films can be rented for three weeks at a charge of about 75 cents. (See chapter on "The Genealogical Library of the Church of Jesus Christ of Latter-Day Saints.")

The Slavic newspaper, the BOHEMIAN DAILY, (published in Racine, Wisconsin from 1861-1918 announced on 5 February 1879, that increased demands on immigrant lines from Hamburg and Bremen permitted a drastic drop in fares. In fact, as early as 1870, an immigrant could come on a single ticket from Prague to Racine for fifty dollars or less.

Through more than two centuries of Austrian domination of Bohemia and Slovakia, many Czechs, Moravians, and Slovaks were converted to Catholicism, often forcibly. Consequently, most of the immigrants in the nineteenth century were Catholics. For the family whose origins you are researching, it can be important to find out where they settled and whether there are any Catholic parishes nearby. If your ancestor attended one of these churches, the minister may have entered the particulars concerning christenings, marriages, and burials of family members, often showing the exact place of origin of the family overseas. The same applies to ancestors of Protestant origin.

One should not overlook the importance of searching cemetery records. Such data can be very valuable for determining the birthplace of individuals and their family connections. Tombstone inscriptions can often yield useful information. However, the sextons keep additional records of information for which there is no room on the tombstones. This information was usually given by close relatives and was quite reliable. Tombstones are sometimes erected several years after burial and give incorrect information. Therefore, it is best to trust the sexton's records. Some sextons do not want to spend the time answering queries, but others go out of their way to accommodate the inquirer. The sexton of the Bohemian National Cemetery in Chicago is one such person. He does considerable research on his own records and is very willing to give as much information as he has.

If you know the place where your immigrant ancestor and his relatives were buried, but do not know the exact cemetery, there are ways of finding this information. The burial may have been in the city cemetery, church burial ground, family farm burial grounds, or minority group burial grounds. The local public library may be able to supply you with a list of the city's cemeteries. It is good to remember to attach a self-addressed, stamped envelope with every inquiry and ask for the charges for the services, although usually there are none.

The information gleaned from the cemetery records can lead to another source, local newspapers. They print obituaries which usually list the remaining relatives of the deceased individual and his place of birth. In addition to the obituaries, the newspapers also print paid death announcements which give similar information. In particular, the staffs of Bohemian and Slovakian language newspapers are often very willing to check the pages of the papers and reproduce the items concerning the immigrant, providing that the applicant supplies them with the date of death (and includes a stamped envelope and minimal fee, usually about $5.00). Again, the local public librarian can give the applicant the names, addresses, and years of establishment of the local Bohemian and Slovakian newspapers. Also the N.W. AYER & SON'S DIRECTORY OF NEWSPAPERS AND PERIODICALS can be checked for more information about local newspapers, such as the possible merger of two or more newspapers in one locality.

Federal or state census records are an excellent source for verifying the residence of the family here in the United States as well as the name of the family head, his occupation, the state or country where he was born, and the amount of cash he owned, and the value of his property. These records also include the names, ages, and states or countries of birth of all who resided with him in the same dwelling. The first census that gives all this information is the census of 1850. The earlier ones are much more limited in the information they record. Since 1790, the federal census has been taken every ten years. With the exception of the census of 1890, which was destroyed by a fire in Washington, D.C., all census records have been preserved. Many public libraries have microfilms of these records including the Latter-Day Saints Genealogical Library. The very helpful 1900 census has not yet been microfilmed since such action needs approval of the Congress. However, all 1900 census records are available through either the National Archives in Washington, D.C. or its branches. The branch locations, their addresses, and states of jurisdiction are given in a very helpful book by James C. and Lila Lee Neagles called LOCATING YOUR IMMIGRANT ANCESTOR--A GUIDE TO NATURALIZATION RECORDS (see bibliography). One of the very helpful features of this 1900 census is that it gives more information concerning citizenship. It indicates whether the individuals are still aliens or become citizens. If the latter, it records the year and the state where the citizenship was granted.

State, county, and city histories are also excellent sources. Biographical sections of these histories contain life stories of many of the first settlers. One might find a story of his ancestor there, or at least people of the same name. These life sketches were often written by the subjects themselves or by members of the family; in short, by whoever knew the details and vital information concerning the subject. The details describing the accomplishments of the individual may be exaggerated, but one can generally assume that factual information about the family history is correct.

It can generally be assumed that those individuals of the same surname in any one locality in the United States all came from the same place in Czechoslovakia. Interviews with the older generation of the family or with the older people of the same surname living in the community where your forefathers settled can often be very productive. Besides their personal knowledge, their mementos and old photographs can frequently yield valuable information. Photographs sometimes give the name and address of the photographer on the reverse side. Other potential sources of information include clippings from American or Czecho-slovakian papers, old letters, or merely envelopes showing the return address or stamp of the post office; old documents, such as birth, marriage or death certificates, that they needed at some time or other to prove their identity to the American authorities, passports; or simply slips of paper with data concerning their relations. Information thus gained can provide a starting point in researching family origins in Czechoslovakia itself. One should be aware, however, that information other than documents may be inaccurate and should be verified from some other source if possible.

Some immigrants are reluctant to reveal any information, saying, "Let the past and the dead be buried undisturbed." There is no cliche that would break down this attitude. We have to admit that not all immigrants came here with spotlessly clean slates. Some of them left as a result of a brush with military or civil authorities and were only too eager to lose themselves and forget about their Czech origins. I remember my own mother, who in reminiscing about some individuals among our acquaintances, would say, "He was a rascal, and he had to leave for America to avoid troubles with the law."

One of the best sources of genealogical information is the individual's application for U.S. citizenship. Many of the immigrants wished to become citizens because they wanted to have legal protection in their adopted country. Of the three documents connected with the naturalization of immigrants (declaration of intention to become a citizen, application for citizenship, and the naturalization certificate) the one that contains the most information is the application, although in varying degrees, since not all the court clerks insisted on having all the data that the forms called for. Also, some applicants had either forgotten or did not know the information being requested. The best source giving details of the complex organization of naturalization records is LOCATING YOUR IMMIGRANT ANCESTOR--A GUIDE TO NATURALIZATION RECORDS by James C. and Lila Lee Neagles.

The records are as authentic, accurate, and helpful as the immigrants could make them. They tried, as they were trained in the "old country," not to attempt to confuse the authorities. However, at times they unwittingly gave confusing or incomplete information. For example, in one instance, the immigrant stated on his application that he was born in Dubrava. This name, as well as his own surname, suggested Slovakia but the Postal Guide lists several Dubravas. Obviously, this information is of little help.

Land records of the place where the immigrants settled can be helpful. Many of the newcomers, lacking funds, took advantage of the Homestead Act, issued on 20 May 1862, through which they could get free land. Under the Homestead Act the applicant had to be an American citizen or prove that he had declared his intentions to become one. The family had to settle on the allotted land, improve it with dwellings and structures for animals, and till the fields. Additional information concerning this can be found in Neagles' book LOCATING YOUR IMMIGRANT ANCESTOR--A GUIDE TO NATURALIZATION RECORDS.

Much valuable information can be gained from wills and deeds. Wills are deposited in the offices of the county clerks. If your Bohemian ancestor made a will, he might have remembered his aged parents, or other relatives that he left behind in his native land. Deeds and records of property transfers are in the offices of the county recorders.

According to the statistics, Czechoslovakian immigration reached its peak in 1907 when 13,554 persons left for the United States. The low ratio of immigrant females to immigrant males created an impression that the Czechoslovak was a shiftless, seasonal migrant, having no intentions to settle permanently. This is simply not true, as later statistics bear out. The Czech immigrant was (and is) at heart a home builder. Too poor to take his wife and children along, the family had to wait until he saved enough to pay for their passage to America, in some instances several years.

To supplement the information given in this section, the reader should also study the chapters on "Names," "Geography," and "Language."

BIBLIOGRAPHY

AMERIKÁN: NÁRODÍ KALENDÁŘ [American, National Calendar]. Chicago: Chicago Daily Svornost, 1873-1957. Published as a yearbook. In Czech.

> The reminiscences of immigrants or their descendants constitute a major body of primary material concerning Czech immigrants in the United States.

BOHEMIANS IN CHICAGO. Chicago Public Library, Toman Branch. 12 vols. Approx. 200 pamphlets.

Capek, Thomas. AMERICAN CZECHS IN PUBLIC OFFICE. Omaha, 1940.

_____. ANCESTRY OF FREDERICK PHILLIPSE. New York; 1939.

_____. AUGUSTINE HERMAN OF BOHEMIA MANOR. Prague: N.p., 1939.

_____. THE CZECH COMMUNITY OF NEW YORK. New York; 1921.

> No data on individuals included.

_____. THE CZECHS (BOHEMIANS) IN AMERICA. American Immigration Series Vol. 11. Reprint. New York: Arno and the New York Times, 1969. GL 973 B4ai.

> A study of the social, cultural, political, economic, and religious life of Czechs in America.

_____. PADESÁT LET ČESKÉHO TISKU V AMERICE. New York; 1911.

> Fifty years of Czech newspapers in America. Important for historical and genealogical research, as it lists numerous Czech periodicals, their history and present deposition.

_____. PAMÁTKY ČESKÝCH EMIGRANTŮ V AMERICE [Memorial of the Czech emigrants in America]. Omaha: Národní Tiskárna, 1907. GL 943.7 W2c or microfilm 896,930 (second item).

> Contribution to the history of the Czech-American immigration.

_____. SLAVS IN THE UNITED STATES CENSUS 1850-1940. Chicago; 1943.

Special reference to Czechoslovakia. Important for demography as it is purely statistical.

CZECH PERIODICALS. University of Illinois Libraries. Slavic and East European collection. Urbana, Champaign, Ill., 61801.

Dobiáš, Josef. NĚMECKÉ OSÍDLENÍ OSTRŮVKU JIHLAVSKÉHO. Prague: Státní archívní škola, 1931. GL 943.723 F2d. In Czech.

Discusses the German settlement of Jihlava (Moravia) district.

Dvořák, Josef. DĚJINY ČECHŮV VE STÁTU SOUTH DAKOTA. South Dakota: Tabor, 1920.

History of the Czechs in the state of South Dakota.

Dvornik, Francis. CZECH CONTRIBUTION TO THE GROWTH OF THE UNITED STATES. Washington, D.C.: By Author, 1961.

Gellner, John and Smerek, John. CZECHS AND SLOVAKS IN CANADA. Toronto: University of Toronto Press, 1968.

Habenicht, J. DĚJINY ČECHŮV AMERICKÝCH. St. Louis; 1904. In Czech.

The history of American Czechs. Since it is an old issue and, consequently, contemporaneous with Czech immigration in the nineteenth century, it probably contains accurate information.

Hudson, Estelle. CZECH PIONEERS IN SOUTHWEST. Dallas; 1934.

Klíma, Stanislav. ČECHOVÉ A SLOVÁCI ZA HRANICEMI. Prague: J. Otto, 1925. GL 943.7 W2k. In Czech.

Czechs and Slovaks abroad. Important contributions of historical and genealogical value.

Ledbetter, Eleanor E. THE CZECHS OF CLEVELAND. Cleveland; 1919.

Luza, Radomir. THE TRANSFER OF SUDETEN GERMANS, 1933-62. New York: University Press, 1964. GL 943.7 H2L.

A study of the Czech-German relationship.

Mallory, Charles Payson. ANCIENT FAMILIES OF BOHEMIA MANOR, THEIR HOMES AND THEIR GRAVES. Wilmington, Delaware: Historical Society of Delaware, 1888.

Moeschler, Felix. GENEALOGICAL NOTES ON FAMILIES FROM HERRNHUT, SAXONY, WHO ORIGINALLY CAME AS RELIGIOUS REFUGEES FROM MORAVIA, BOHEMIA, AUSTRIA AND SILESIA. 2 vols. Herrnhut, 1933. GL 943.212 D2m.

Molique, Thelma D.H. AUGUSTINE HERRMAN, 1605-1686: FIRST
FOREIGNER EVER NATURALIZED IN AMERICA IN 1673. N.p., n.d.
GL 929.273 AL no. 479 or microfilm 897,280 (3d item).

Neagles, James C. and Lila Lee. LOCATING YOUR IMMIGRANT
ANCESTOR--A GUIDE TO NATURALIZATION RECORDS. Logan, Utah:
Everton Publishers, 1975.

> A guide to naturalization records.

PANORAMA. Chicago: Czechoslovak National Council of America, 1974.

> A historical review of Czechs and Slovaks in the
> United States. Contains numerous biographies.

Rosicky, Rose. HISTORY OF CZECHS IN NEBRASKA. Omaha, 1929.
GL 978.2 F2r.

> Contains numerous biographies and necrologies.

Roucek, Josef. CZECHS AND SLOVAKS IN AMERICA. Cultural
Mosaic Series. Lerner Publication, 1967.

Schacherl, Lilian. WEGE INS EXIL. Graefeling bei Muenchen:
N.p., 1964. GL 943.7 W2s. In German.

> Famous refugees of Bohemia and Moravia.

Vlček, F.J. NÁŠ LID V AMERICE [Our people in America].
Týn n/Vlt., Czechoslovakia: N.p., 1935. In Czech.

> Valuable for genealogical research.

Articles and Dissertations

Bicha, Karel D. "The Czechs in Wisconsin history" WISCONSIN
MAGAZINE OF HISTORY, 53, no. 3 (1970): 194.

"Catholic Holy Cross Cemetery, San Francisco." In BALKAN
AND EASTERN EUROPEAN AMERICAN GENEALOGICAL AND HISTORICAL
SOCIETY, (1967), p.21.

> Copies of tombstones, 1920-30, of Romanians, Alban-
> ians, Galicians, Czechoslovaks, Croatians, Slovenians,
> Serbians, Yugoslavians, Dalmatians, Austrians. Ages
> given.

Hrbková, Sárka. "Bohemians in Nebraska." NEBRASKA STATE
HISTORICAL SOCIETY. Omaha 9:140. GL 978.2 B5o.

Martinek, Josef. "Czechoslovak Ingredients in the Melting
Pot." AMERICAN-CZECHOSLOVAK FLASHES 15 Oct. 1947.

Mecenseffy, Grete. CENTRAL EUROPEAN POPULATION MOVEMENTS. The World Conference on Records and Genealogical Seminar, D-12, Salt Lake City: Church of Jesus Christ of Latter-Day Saints, 1969. GL 929.1 W893.

   The lecture concerns all central European countries. Important demographic information.

Sartan, Y. "One Czech Immigrant." KANSAS HISTORICAL SOCIETY COLLECTIONS 8 (1913-14): 471,506.

   Does not refer to any particular person.

Taggart, Glen L. "Czechs of Wisconsin as a Cultural Type." Ph.D. dissertation, University of Wisconsin, 1948.

Chapter 5
SOURCES FOR GENEALOGICAL RESEARCH IN CZECHOSLOVAKIA

The Czechs and Moravians have always been a record-keeping people with kroniky (chronicles) having been kept by families, clans, villages, or regions. Although most of the chronicles have been lost through the ages, some have survived to the present. Family Bibles record births, marriages, and death, and personal chronicles record the circumstances surrounding these events, often as they related to the happenings in their nation.

Numerous sources can be employed in Czech genealogical research. Church records are particularly valuable. Vital information such as christenings, marriages, and burials were all carefully recorded by the priest in the church books. Details of business agreements had to be listed in the Pozemkové knihy (land books). Because many records were kept, these varied sources have been collected into the Oblastní Archívy (District Archives), Státní Archívy (State Archives), or into the archives of individual cities or institutions. There they have been carefully sorted and many of them indexed and catalogued. Fortunately, there are only a few of these sources which are considered restricted and, for one reason or another, are not available to the public for research.

Before these sources are discussed, it should be pointed out that some are primary sources and others secondary sources and their value should be judged accordingly.

VITAL RECORDS

Prior to 1869-70, only the matriky (registers of the churches) contained the records of births, christenings, marriages, and deaths, and burials. In 1869, some ministers refused to perform and record the marriages of those people who were not Roman Catholic. For this and other reasons, the function of matriky was taken over by local civic officials. The Catholic Church, as well as other churches, still had the right to record the ordinances and keep the records; however, only the books of the local (town or city) officials were considered valid and legal. These records are in possession of the Místní Národní Výbor (Local National Committee).

A program for the keeping of vital statistics on a state basis was introduced in 1921 and revised in 1949. These statistics consist of reports from physicians attending births or deaths, and from reports of civil authorities concerning marriages and divorces performed in their jurisdiction. Anyone who needs a document concerning an event subsequent to 1869-70 can apply for a copy through the Embassy of the Czechoslovak Socialist Republic (Consular division, 3900 Linnean Ave., N.W., Washington, D.C., 20008). The fee is $6.00, prepaid and is subject to change. The certificates are made in Czechoslovakia and thus are in the Czech or Slovak languages only. (The embassy is not in a position to assist in the translation of these documents.)

In order to make it possible for the officials to locate and identify the entry in their records, it is important that the researcher submit the following minimum information: (1) the exact place of the event (birth, marriage, or death), (2) if not exact date, at least the year of the event, and (3) the name by which the person was known in Czechoslovakia. To obtain the birth or marriage certificate of a woman, the maiden name is necessary. Any correspondence with the Czechoslovakian Embassy in Washington, D.C. can be conducted in English. Be sure to include your name and address.

If the information given by the researcher is insufficient and the document is not found, a charge will still be made. For example, no search can be made for the birth date of a person whom the applicant identifies simply as being born "close to Prague." There are many subdivisions located in larger cities and in their environs. To search them all would entail considerable time and expense.

Vital records are considered a primary source inasmuch as they were reported by an eyewitness present at the time of the event. However, the researcher should be cautioned that statements relating to the age of a person at the time of marriage or death are not always correct. Individuals being married did not always give their true age; or the person giving the information for a person who died often had to guess the age.

Birth records may include the name of the child; date and place of the birth; full names of the parents; the occupation(s), residence, ages, and names of their parents; names of witnesses and their relationship to the parents; and the name of the midwife.

Records of marriages may include the date and the place of the marriage; full names of the bride and the groom, their ages and places of birth and occupations; whether widower or widow; and full names of their parents and their residence.

Death records are usually much briefer. They contain the date and place of death, full name of the deceased (in the case of a female they might give her maiden name), age at death, and the name of the spouse or parents.

MATRIKY (CHURCH RECORDS)

Inasmuch as the matriky are by far the most frequently used sources of information in ancestral research in Czechoslovakia, and also because of the large amount of data they offer, they will be analyzed here in detail.

While most of the ancient records of the Church of United Brethren have been destroyed, some of the oldest Catholic Church records have been preserved. These fragments include the book of christenings in Horní Jiretín by the city of Most for the year 1441; in the Svatý Tomáš (St. Thomas) parish in Prague in 1500; and Nejdek, 1557 and Aberthamy by Nejdek for 1545.

In Moravia, the oldest registers preserved are the parishes of Svatý Jakub in Brno for 1587, Svatý Jakub in Jihlava for 1599, and fragments of a few others. As a rule, none of these give the names of the parents when listing the christening of a child.

The Catholic Council in Trent in 1563 ordered registers to designate christenings and marriages. The Ritual Romanorum of 16 June 1614 decreed that the registration of death should also be included.

After the brutal takeover of the České Země by the Hapsburgs in 1620, only the Catholic Church was allowed to keep books. In 1605 the Prague Synod specifically ordered that the christenings and marriages be kept in one book and confirmations in another. The latter listed the full name of the confirmee, and one can only assume that at the time of the ordination the person was at least twelve years of age.

The old matriky are in the form of long narrow pages; frequently they were loose and were bound together later. Often the pages were divided into columns for various items of information with each entry numbered. If the minister had several villages within the jurisdiction of the parish, he would travel to each of these, frequently accompanied by someone else who was acquainted with the art of writing and who could assist in recording the events. This explains the variety of writing in these books and also why, at times, the books were not deposited in the minister's office. One single matrika might be divided into sections according to the villages for which the minister was responsible. Průvodce po Státním Archivu (see section on Státní Oblastní Archívy, pp. 72-73) is of an invaluable help at this point as it lists the villages that are within the jurisdiction of each parish. More will be said about these archival guides later.

Conversely, a matrika might record christenings, marriages, and deaths in chronological order, disregarding distinctions of the smaller locality. The keepers of the matriky, in addition to the required entries, often added information concerning special events, such as fires, floods, or murders. In addition, the recorder frequently inserted folksy re-marks--songs which the young men sang on the village square in the evening hours, or popular, witty sayings.

Emperor Joseph II (1741-90) introduced a prescribed form for the matriky and ordered that the records of christenings list full names of both parents and both sets of grand-parents, occupation, and the conscription number of the house of the family residence. These new items made the subsequent matriky more valuable for genealogical research. They not only furnished a proof of an individual's brothers and sisters, but also helped to establish a link between generations. Joseph II also ordered the use of Latin or German in lieu of Czech. Many priests preferred Latin to the German language.

Until the nineteenth century, the matriky did not list dates of births and deaths. All the dates shown are the dates of christenings and burials. Surnames are listed for parents but not for the infant unless he was illegiti-mate.

In 1771, the Protestants were allowed to keep their own rec-ords, but they had to submit them to the Catholic priests. This resulted in an interesting situation as the Catholic matriky contained many Protestant marriages. It was not, however, the Protestant practice to have babies christened, thus their children were not included in the registers of the Catholic Church nor their own church. It is possible that these children may appear in the books of the Protes-tant church merely as a listing of membership growth.

The Patent of Toleration, a most important document, was issued by Joseph II on 1 May 1781. This document extended the rights of Protestant (evangelic) churches to worship openly and to keep their own books, though still under the supervision of the Catholic Church. In addition to this patent, on 20 February 1784, the emperor recognized the importance of the matriky, which up to then were considered the private property of the church.

In January 1790, an order was issued which required that al the matriky be indexed. In 1802 this order was made retro-active and applied to all the older books as well. There is no guarantee that these indexes are accurate or complete. We suggest that if the given name of a person does not appear in the index, a search be made in the matrika itself on and around the date of the event.

In 1799, the priests were required to prepare copies of their books, old and current, and submit them to the consistory of the bishop. Many of these copies have been preserved where originals were destroyed. However, because of the errors made during the copying process, caution must be exercised in their use.

All the laws, orders, and rules mentioned here were very beneficial for the keeping of the church records, statistics for the state, for individuals or families that needed a valid proof of an event and now for genealogical researchers. Indeed, they were extremely helpful provided the ministers and other keepers of the matriky understood them properly and were ready and willing to follow them in detail. Under ideal conditions the matriky are considered a primary source. If no other record contradicts the entries, they should be accepted even if they are seemingly incorrect. To instigate a correction in the matriky, one would have to bring to the officials a legal, valid proof for the change. As far as accepting the entries as given in the matriky, which would extend the ancestry for another generation, one has to consider many factors and clues, drawing on experience and also on the knowledge of the old language.

When entering the christening of an illegitimate child, it was forbidden to list the name of the father unless he specifically admitted his fatherhood. Times and the so-called men of God were cruel to the illegitimate child and its mother. In the matrika of Přeslavice there is the following entry on 28 July 1658, "christened child Filip from Javornice; father fuc (the modern English equivalent would be the vernacular "he split"); mother, a bad monkey." Or the entry was simply recorded as "spratek, parchant" (bastard); "father does not exist," "father disorderly," or christened "from the left hip." This last entry, no doubt, refers to the child of a nobleman. At times the name of such a father was given, but he did not suffer any adverse consequences. Sometimes the priests tried to inject a little bit of humor and further humiliate the mother by adding "father drowned in the mud puddle," "father drowned in summer under the ice," "father drowned in the puddle behind the kitchen stove." Whether the name of the father was known or not, illegitimate children went through life under the surname of the mother.

At the beginning of the seventeenth century there was a dire need for Catholic priests. Many of the oldest parishes were assigned to foreign ministers, such as the Poles or Germans. It was easy for them to misunderstand names and other information given by people who were illiterate and therefore enter it in their books incorrectly. Even the Czech priests did not always understand the real purpose of the registers, and so they often did not pay attention to the proper spelling of the name, correct occupation, age, and residence of the persons involved. In particular, information connected with a burial was often omitted, especially if the deceased was a person of lower status.

Frequently the minister would enter only the date and such meager data as "a servant died," "a child of a smith was buried," and so forth. Often the entry was made a few days after the event, particularly if the occasion was celebrated boisterously in true Czech fashion. This would have included the priest who may not have been able to wake up from the excessive drinking until a day or two after the celebration; he would then record only what he remembered-- right or wrong.

Ages of the parents recorded at the time of a christening, a marriage, or a burial may be in error since the parents often did not even know how old they really were. The surnames and given names could also be given in different variations, depending on the language used--Czech, Latin, or German. Nicknames were sometimes used for given names, for example, Marie could be found entered as Maria, Marí, Mariana, Marjána, or Marka.

In Slovakia there are only a few registers extant from the sixteenth or seventeenth centuries. Many were lost during the Turkish invasions and the Slovak rebellions in the seventeenth and eighteenth centuries. Protestants and Catholics began to keep registers at about the same time, but more of the Protestant books have been preserved from the early period because at the turn of the seventeenth century the ruling regime leaned toward the Lutheran Refor- mation. In the former Hungary up to 1610, neither church had an independent organization, but each was subordinated to the hierarchy of the Roman Catholic church. Their matriky were periodically inspected by the Catholic offi- cials. During the religious wars in the seventeenth centu- ry, Catholics and Protestants frequently replaced each other in the parishes, depending on the religious affiliation of the estate nobleman, who, as a patron of the Church, had the right to dictate the religion of his subjects. In 1670 a powerful movement toward Catholicism began; conse- quently, in the second half of the century, most of the higher nobility turned to Catholicism. This had an effect on the religion of the whole area as well as on the matriky.

In 1649 the Greek Catholic church was organized by a union of the Russian Orthodox and Roman Catholic churches. Under this arrangement the patents of Maria Theresia and Joseph II given to the Czech lands concerning the keeping of the matriky and their legal status extended also to the churches in Hungary, under the rule of which Slovakia was at that time.

The matriky of Protestant churches were written in the Slo- vak language as early as 1720. Prior to 1720, Hungarian was used and after 1780 the Latin language crept in. This usage remained until 1840 when a statute was issued pre- scribing the use of Hungarian, even in the localities where no Hungarian nationals resided. Another statute in 1868 allowed religious groups to keep their registers in the language mostly used in the area of the denomination, for example, the Greek Catholic church used Cyrillic.

As early as the seventeenth century, Jews were required to report their marriages, births, and deaths to the Catholic minister for recording in the <u>matriky</u>. These entries were usually listed on the few last pages. The responsibility for the correctness of the entry belonged to the priest. Very often, however, he was not given the true data. This information was used for the purposes of military conscription, so that the Jews would often report the birth of a son as that of a daughter. This is the reason why there were so few Jews in the military service. Frequently they gave the wrong residence or surname.

Originally Jews did not have surnames, which led to many legal complications. Early in the eighteenth century, under Maria Theresia, they were ordered to report to the magistrates and register a surname, with the understanding that from then on they would be known by such registered surnames. The Jews who could afford a bribe were allowed dignified surnames, all in German. When the poor Jew did not pay, he received a humiliating surname, such as Vocásek (little tail); Bulík (stupid as an ox); or Trouba (dumb). Frequently the surnames were even obscene.

Jewish rabbis kept their own records, such as the book of the circumsized. As a result of the Theresian and Josephinian reforms, the keeping of general registers for Jews was introduced. In 1766, individual synagogues were ordered to keep registers concerning Jewish males. Birth registers for Jewish females were introduced only in 1783. These registers received legal status in 1868-70 after passage of the laws concerning the keeping of vital records.

The Jewish registers were subjected to stricter regulations than those of other denominations, as the Jews differed from other churches concerning which events should be recorded and how. The recording of weddings was under dispute, as the Jews believed that marriage is a civil matter not requiring the services of a rabbi.

There are few sources for tracing the genealogy of individual Jewish families to the period earlier than the eighteenth century. Most of them are incomplete, indefinite, and almost inaccessible.

The names of some Jewish families or individuals can be found in the registers of the Bohemian Chancery from the years 1527-1746, which contain conscription orders concerning Jews.

Documents of the Commissions on Jews, which were established during the reduction of Jews in Bohemia, are another source. This file first became active 11 August 1679. It included various documents, for example, the requests of Jews for

consent of marriage; dispensation for "incolatus" (citizenship, residency, domicile, aliens in permanent residence
without citizenship); censuses of the Jews living in rural
areas from the year 1724, of the Prague Jews from the year
1729; four books with indexes of permission to marry for
Jews from 1715-1825; the census of Jewish families living
in Bohemia from the year 1799; the census of Jewish families
from the year 1811; catastres concerning Jews for the entire country of Bohemia from the year 1811. Altogether,
these documents comprise 180 volumes.

By the decree of 1784 of Joseph II, a continuous series was
created, containing listings on Jews, files for diverse
proceedings, taxes and miscellaneous accounts, and govern-
mental administrative material.

When the Jews became full citizens of the České Země in
1867, the files covering Jewish affairs gradually became
integrated with other official, judicial, administrative,
and private records and were no longer kept separately.

Under the German occupation during World War II, when the
Jews were so severely persecuted, the Nazis required many
Czech citizens, if they wished to avoid persecution, to
prove that they were not Jewish by reconstructing their
ancestry for three generations. To avoid irregularities
and changes of entries, the Nazi regime ordered the records
of all the synagogues to be concentrated in Prague. Consequently, all the Jewish records are presently stored at
the Obvodní Národní Výbor, Matriční oddělení, Prague I,
Vodičkova 18, Czechoslovakia. There is no printed inventory of the collection; however, the director has on hand
a temporary, typewritten directory. The earliest date is
probably 1730. Stored in the same area with these records
are the registers listing the names of Czechoslovakian
Jews who died in the Nazi concentration camps during the
Second World War. It is difficult to determine the religious jurisdiction of the locality where the Jewish ancestors resided; so it is suggested that the information be
given to the Czechoslovakian Embassy, (3900 Linnean Ave.,
N.W., Washington, D.C., 20008) with a request for help in
determining the closest synagogue.

The following abbreviations are used in the records to
denote various churches:

     R.K.   Roman Catholic
     Ev.A.C. Protestant, Augsburg Confession
     Ev.Ref. Reformed Protestant
     Izr.   Jewish

Almost all the church books other than those of the Jews
are deposited in the Oblastní Archívy throughout the
Republic and contain records from the beginnings of the
various parishes up to and including the year 1870. In
Slovakia the matriky covering the period to 1899 are in
Státnych Archívoch. With the exception of Slovakia, a
register which contains entries from the time before 1870

and also after 1870, would be found in the Oblastní Archív. As of this writing there still are some registers that have not been deposited there, especially in Slovakia, but ultimately they should all reside in the Oblastní Archívy.

SČÍTÁNÍ LIDU (CENSUS RETURNS)

A population count has been taken through history by many countries for various reasons. In the majority of cases the rulers simply wanted to know the population total for purposes of taxation and military conscription. The results of such censuses are of tremendous value for the study of demography.

For locating the residence of the ancestral family, the genealogist could find no better tool than the Sčítání lidu if it is detailed enough. For many centuries Czechoslovakia was under the feudal system, and the information found in Sčítání lidu, or similar sources that have the appearance of census returns, was of the utmost importance to the estate owners or lords. The population of these estates were obligated to labor for the lord; thus the lords had to know the number and the age of the males on whom they could rely for tilling the lands and accomplishing other chores. This he accomplished by his own counts of the population. Even though such records are not classified as official Sčítání lidu, they have been included in this chapter because of their importance to genealogists.

Censuses, 1158 and on

This is a very vague description of the sources; but then, the records themselves are very vague. In many instances only fragments were preserved nor were the accounts always taken uniformly and systematically. They were taken solely for the purposes of taxation and statistics. For the most part their value is greater for the historian or demographer than for the genealogist. These records are deposited at the National Archives in Prague and form an inseparable part of the feudal records. These records are completely in Latin. No inventory for the public use has been prepared.

Soupis Obyvatelstva v Čechách, 1651 (Census Of Population, 1651)

The Austrian Hapsburgs dominated the České Země after the Battle of the White Mountain in 1620. The census of 1651 was taken as part of the catholicization of the population in Bohemia. The main purpose of this census was to establish whether the people were members of the favorite Catholic Church and whether there was any hope that they might become Catholic. This census, however incomplete, benefited both the landlords and government as information regarding the estimation of prospective labor forces and as a guide for tax assessment. The order was revoked later

the same year. The following is a sample of the information that the census offers.

Jmena lidi	Stav	Kdo a jakeno povolani	V letech	Katolicky	Ne katolicky	Nadeje jeho ziskani	Zadne nadeje
Ves Holejsov:							
Jakub Holejsovsky	svobodny	robotny	50	/	/	/	
Rozina	svobodna	manzelka	40		/	/	
Jan	svobodny	syn	16	/		/	
Simon	svobodny	pacholek	15		/	/	
Markyta	svobodna	devka	30		/	/	
Adam Holejsovsky	svobodny	chalupnik	50	/		/	
Dorota	svobodna	manzelka	35		/	/	
Jirik	svobodny	syn	18	/			
Jirik Holejsovsky	svobodny	podruh	55		/	/	
Anna	svobodna	manzelka	40		/	/	
Vavrinec Holejsovsky	svobodny	chalupnik	37		/	/	
Katerina	svobodna	manzelka	28		/	/	
Mikolas Holejsovsky	svobodny	podruh	25		/	/	
Zuzana	svobodna	matka	56		/	/	
Jan Zeman	svobodny	podruh	40	/			
Katerina	svobodna	manzelka	50	/	/	/	
Katerina	svobodna	dcera	20				

Meaning of the titles of the columns:

    Jména Lidí (names of the people)
    Stav (status)

Although in this sample there are frequent entries "svobodný" (free), that does not necessarily mean that the individual was free of the vassal obligation. He was probably
free as far as his stay on the local estate is concerned.

    Kdo jest a jakého povolání (occupation)
    V letech (approximate age)
    Katolický (Catholic)
    Naděje na jeho získání (hope for his conversion)
    Žádná naděje (no hope)

Translations of the expressions in the third column:

    robotný (vassal)
    manzelka (wife)
    syn (son)

```
pacholek (male servant)
děvka (female servant)
chalupnik(cottager)
podruh (laborer)
matka (mother)
dcera (daughter)
```

A researcher, whose ancestral family lived in Bohemia in
the year 1651, can inquire--through the services of the
Czechoslovakian Embassy in Washington, D.C.--whether such
a census schedule was prepared and is extant and available
for the village where his forefathers resided. This very
valuable source is deposited in the Archives of the Ministry
of Interior. No indexes for public information have been
prepared.

On 13 October 1753, an imperial order for all Austrian lands
was issued which required that lists be made of all individuals in the country. This included the České Země. The
resulting account served only military purposes. The populace was classified according to age, sex and marital status. Classification by age was: 1 to 15 years, 15 to 20
years, 20 to 40 years, 40 to 50 years, and over 50 years
of age.

In the following year, 1754, two decrees were issued by
Empress Maria Theresia, the first on 19 January and the
second on 16 February. The latter decree altered the time
period for which this list would be compiled, from every
year to every three years. Under another decree of 22 May
1762, an additional rubric entitled "occupation" was added
to the classification of the populace. Also, an annual
census was ordered. The results of these censuses are
preserved only in summaries, partly in central archives,
partly in contemporary published literature. It is not
known whether any of the locally compiled lists have been
preserved.

In 1770 a census was carried out with the cooperation of
military authorities. In it was included conscription
lists of the male population and draft animals. No one
was permitted to leave an induction district without permission. The only exception to this rule applied to persons of the free estates and the nobility and the clergy.

Aside from the summary figures, only two census schedules
from this period are known to have been preserved, one is
of Prague, the Old City (Praha - Staré Město) and the other
is of Prague, the New City (Praha - Nové Město). Both
lists are deposited in the Prague city archives. The census schedule of Old Prague has appeared in print (Šebesta
Eduard and Adolf Ludvík Krejčík, POPIS OBYVATELSTVA HLAVN-
ÍHO MĚSTA PRAHY, I, STARÉ MĚSTO, 1770 Vol. 23 [Prague:
Československá rodopisná společnost, 1933]). This book
is available in the Genealogical Library of the Latter-Day
Saints Church in Salt Lake City, Utah, (call no. 943.715 X2p).

The compilers have done an excellent job in preparing a complete name index and also transposing the numerous abbreviations into full meanings. The material is divided into sections of streets and public squares. Some of the entries are most interesting and give a lot of valuable information. For example, Cossovinus Leine, laborer of Offerten in Clevsko (?) now settled here (B); sons: Karel 6 years, Michal 2 years and Frantisek 1/2 year (all E). Letter "B" signifies that the individual is physically not capable to bear arms and letter "E" means that the person in the future can be inducted into military service.

The remnant of such a valuable record is very important to the genealogist. As early as 1770, Prague was a large city with many parishes. One who traces his ancestry to Prague faces the very difficult task of searching through the various parishes to find records of his family. This printed census schedule of males living in 1770 in Staré Mĕsto can help the researcher establish the parish where the family resided.

The census, in the modern sense of the word, begins only in 1805. The oldest lists are in book form, organized alphabetically by last name. Entries within this division were made according to the conscription number of the houses. House conscription numbers were arranged according to the time of their construction rather than by their location in the community. In 1805 the houses were generally given new conscription district numbers, which are in use even at the present time. This change is extremely important for the genealogist. Prior to 1805, the matriky also gave the house conscription number, which provides reliable information for connecting individuals with particular families. In searching for the ancestor after 1805, one should be aware of this change and proceed with caution in linking families through the house conscription number.

Conscription lists have been preserved sporadically; the officials themselves did not realize their value and often allowed them to be destroyed. Those extant are deposited in the city archives, or, where the city archives do not exist as separate institutions, in the appropriate division of the Oblastní Archívy.

The last Austrian census for the České Zemé was prepared in 1910. In the Czechoslovakian Republic the first census originated in 1921. Although originally deposited in the Ministry of Interior in Prague, the results were divided among various Oblastní Archívy in 1952. They are arranged according to the former judicial districts and individual political units (cities and villages). The 1921 census included the name, sex, marital status, relationship to the head of the family, age, place and date of birth, nationality, religion, occupation, length of residence in the locality, capacity to read and write, and the name of the employer.

The archives of the city of Prague contain veritable trea-
sures of old Sčitáni lidu or other similar documents. Among
the oldest ones are old census returns. The old census
returns were usually arranged according to the sections of
the city and were not taken at the same time in each division. In Prague, the New City (Nové Město) the first book
dates back to 1811-12; in Prague, the Old City (Staré Město)
to 1814 and in Hradčany and Malá Strana to the 1820s. All
include both surname and given name, and residence street
address. Somewhat later, the given names of the wives and
their birth dates were also included.

The census schedules between 1825-40 contain (with varying
degrees of completeness) the full names of the husband and
wife, the years of their births, their birthplaces, occupations, present residence, sometimes the wife's maiden
name and her father's name, and the year of marriage. The
census schedules after 1870 contain names and years of
birth of all members of the household, plus their occupations and birthplaces, often their marriage dates, moves
in the past, and deaths of the members of the family and
so forth.

All census returns are considered primary sources as far
as the family relationship and names of the individuals are
concerned. They cannot be considered primary sources for
information on ages unless the full birthdate is given.
Fortunately, this often is the case.

In Slovakia, the census was taken according to the Hungarian
laws. In the nineteenth century the years of the census
were 1869, 1880, and 1890; and in the twentieth century,
1910. The results are deposited in Hungary (Magyar Ors-
zágos Levertár-i, Budapest I, Becsi kapu tér 4). When
Slovakia became the part of the Czechoslovakian republic,
the census was taken in 1920, 1930 and then, separately
for the České Země in 1940. Material gathered in the 1920
census for the whole republic is deposited in the Ustredni
Archiv in Prague, while the 1920 and 1940 Slovakian censuses are in Státný Slovenský Ustredný Archiv in Bratislava.
Thus far the services of the Czechoslovakian Embassy in
Washington, D.C., do not include searches of the census
schedules.

The Genealogical Department of the Church of Jesus Christ
of Latter-Day Saints has microfilmed the majority of the
Hungarian records, including the 1869 census. Those areas
of Slovakia that became part of the Czechoslovakian republic
after 1918 are included in this census. The reference to
these can be found in the card catalogue of the Genealogical Library in the Czechoslovakian collection. The information in the 1869 census returns is extremely detailed,
with each page or section devoted to only one house,
whether one or several families are in residence. One can
find the following information listed: full name, sex, year
and place of birth, religion, marital status, occupation,

whether local resident or not, length of residence, whether the person writes or reads, and any special remarks (for example, retired military man).

Robotní Seznamy or Soupisy Poddaných (Lists of vassals)

There was no set time for preparation of these lists; the decision for making them depended entirely on the needs of the local landlord or estate owner. It was in his interest to have a complete list of the males who could be recruited for mandatory labor on his estate, not only at present, but also in the future. The following is an example of such Soupis poddaných in the Jarošov nad Nežárkou, prepared in 1760:

> Bartl KOSAR, 38 years, wife 28 years, 2 children.
> Tomáš UCHYTIL, 30, wife 37, 3 children by V. BUZEK.
> Ondřej SKALA, 63, wife 39, 2 children, 13 and 12.

The robotní seznamy are valuable because they list the ages of the couple, which is necessary for further research. They are deposited in the Oblastní Archívy (see the chapter on "Archives"). However, robotní seznamy are listed among the papers and documents of estates, rather than those of the villages. Thus, one would have to know which estate the ancestral village belonged to. Local archivists have lists of villages for every estate within their district.

POSLEDNÍ VŮLE—TESTAMENT (LAST WILL)

This document and others included in the probate records are not very popular sources for genealogical research in Czechoslovakia. The local experts will tell you that there is no need to search the probate records since the matriky are such complete sources and give more detailed information. In addition, the depository of the Poslední vůle is difficult to locate and accessible only for legal purposes which have to be attested to by a lawyer. Thus the information one might find in such uncertain documents would be very expensive indeed.

In ancient times, and even quite recently, the handshake between two or more parties in České Země, as well as in Slovakia, was as binding as a signed paper. According to village traditions, property, identified by the conscription number, usually went to the eldest son, who in turn, took care of the parents when they no longer were able to labor on the farm. Their status was called "vyménkaři" (retired). The daughters received a dowry at the time of their marriage, and the younger sons--nothing. When the father was well-to-do, an agreement was sometimes made to set up the unfortunate younger sons in some trade or business. If all else failed, they had their wives' dowries to fall back on.

Nobility, moneyed, or other important people who made wills
had them recorded and kept at the Státní Notářství (State
Notary) in each district. Recently they have been collected
in the Oblastní Archívy but are not presently available for
research. The purpose of the offices of the notary was to
prepare public papers, wedding contracts, last wills, and
so forth. The files of a retiring or deceased notary were
closed and deposited at the county court in the Notarial
Archive. Recently they became a part of the holdings of
the Oblastní Archívy (see chapter on "Archives"). The offices of notaries were established 29 September 1850, and
the system dissolved in 1949.

VOJENSKÉ ZÁZNAMY (MILITARY RECORDS)

The military records originated quite early, but those
which have been preserved are fragmentary at best. Though
some records reach back to the Thirty Years' War (following
1620), most are subsequent to 1764. These records consist
of 2 main categories: church registers and records of
regiments.

The entries in the military church registers are as complete
as any Catholic Church book. In the year 1768 field chap-
lains were given the responsibility for keeping books.
However, a child of a military couple could have been christened by the army chaplain and by the local church priest
as well. The event would be recorded in both military and
local matriky. The entry in the local matriky would show
a note that the father was in the service, even naming the
regiment. In 1816, duplicate copies of military records were
prepared. These and other records prior to 1918 are deposited at the Apostolic Vicariat in Vienna, Austria. The
original records from Bohemia and Moravia up to about 1870
and from Slovakia from the beginning until discontinuation
in 1949, are preserved in the Institute of Military History
in Prague. The original registers from České Země after
1870 have been deposited in the Archive of the District
National Committee in Prague I. ("I" designates a section
of Prague.)

Either category of military records, that is the church
registers or those of the regiments, are in better order
than any other record, as the old Austrian military was
very exact in keeping track of every individual in service.
Unfortunately, none of them are available for genealogical
research at the present time. If, in the future, they do
become accessible, one will have to know the regiment or
branch of service to which the ancestor belonged in order
to locate the information about him in the military records.

LAND RECORDS

Land records include a variety of books. If located and properly interpreted, they constitute a valuable source for genealogical research, often providing a better link with the distant past than any other document (record) available.

Zemské Desky (Landtafeln in German, Libri Citatonium in Latin, Land Tablets in English)

The original Zemské Desky were written records of court matters initiated by the nobility and heard before the Zemský soud (the highest court). The Bohemian Zemské Desky developed as early as the thirteenth century, but most of these early books were destroyed in the Prague castle fire of 1541. An attempt has been made to reconstruct the Bohemian Zemské Desky from copies deposited elsewhere. This incomplete collection is on file at the Státní Ustřední Archív in Prague. With the passage of time, other books were created to record specific transactions by the nobility, called quaterns. The quaterns include records of purchases, cessions, and exchanges of free estates. There are also special entries concerning other subjects of the king besides the nobility; and, since 1755, Jewish land dealings are included.

The Bohemian quaterns are preserved in the historical division of the Prague central archives. The earliest Moravian Zemské Desky date from 1348 and are deposited in the highest court in Brno.

Patrimoniální Knihy (Patrimonial Books)

While the Zemské Desky concern the nobility, the Patrimoniální Knihy pertain to the vassals. Such books were kept for each estate or domain in Bohemia. They begin in the second half of the fifteenth century and are older than the matriky. Originally, these books noted the changes in the ownership of individual estates and the income which proceeded from such transactions. Often they also contained a list of vassals and the taxes paid by them. Later, the Patrimonial books also included lists of the inhabitants of the estates, testaments, debts, orphan matters, mortgages, marriage contracts, inheritance, and other matters. The completeness of these records depended on the talent and inclination of the bookkeeper.

The Patrimoniální Knihy are kept in the state archives. In only a few instances are individual books preserved in the archives of a lower jurisdiction, such as the Oblastní or City Archives. In some cases, archives of prominent noble families have been kept intact in the offices of the estate or in other local depositories. Curators of the Oblastní Archív would have knowledge concerning the location of particular estate Patrimoniální Knihy.

Berní Ruly (Catastrum Rollare in Latin; Tax Lists in English)

The Berní Ruly are lists of tax payers based on the records of the estate owners or nobility. First completed in 1654, they are considered one of the most important sources for the study of demography.

The tax system before 1654 was not always administered impartially. Tradesmen and owners of small farms were often taxed not only by the lords but also by the state and the Catholic Church. The lords, meanwhile, felt that as free people they were also free from tax obligations. The villages were assessed taxes according to the number of dwellings. Whenever an owner of a small plot of property died and left no legal heirs, the property fell to the lords. However, the taxes on the property and its dwellings were not paid by the lords, but assumed by the remaining village population.

These and other conditions prompted the Czech parliament in 1652 to form a commission of 12 members, composed of representatives of 4 estates: the clergy, nobility, knighthood and burghers. This commission was charged with the responsibility of studying the inequities of the tax structure, verifying the statements of the lords and then making appropriate adjustments. They worked with the "přiznávací listy," or declaration certificates, prepared by the lords; and in most instances they made a personal check of the dwellings, fields, and animals of the taxpayers. The survey was completed in 1654. Other surveys were made in 1683-84, 1746, 1757 and 1792. Although the primary importance of the Berní Rula for genealogical research lies in the possibility of locating the domicile of one's ancestor, it cannot be considered as a complete survey of the population. The Berní Rula did not include the poor who were without property or trade. In addition, only the heads of families were listed, and no indication was made of the number of dependents.

Many Berní Rulas for various counties in Bohemia have been published by the Státní pedagogické nakladatelství in Prague and have been purchased by the Genealogical Library (their collective number is 943.7 B4b). The following is an account of each volume:

Volume 1. Introduction to the series Berní Rula. Written in 1950.

Volume 2. Doskočil Karel. POPIS ČECH, 1654. Souhrnný popis obcí, osad a samot. 1654. Printed in 1953-54. Index to all villages, settlements and hamlets in 1654. Includes lists of nobility, also German names for the localities in Bohemia.

Volume 3. Líva, Václav: PRAŽSKÁ MĚSTA. Printed in 1949. Includes directory of property owners.

Volume 4-7. <u>Bechynsky county</u>. Not published yet.

Volume 8-9. <u>Boleslavsky county</u>. Not published yet.

Volume 10-11. Beneš, E. ČÁSLAVSKO. Printed in 1953, 1955. County Čáslav.

Volume 12-15. Pešák, Vaclav. KRAJ HRADECKÝ. Printed in 1951, 1954. Incomplete. Only vol. 12 and 13 in the GL. County Hradec Králové, Bohemia.

Volume 16-17. <u>Chrudim county</u>. Not published yet.

Volume 18-19. Haasová, Marie (Jelínkova). KRAJ KOUŘIMSKÝ. Printed in 1951. County Kouřim.

Volume 20-21. Litoměřicko. <u>County Litoměřice.</u> Not yet published.

Volume 22. Loketsko. <u>County of Loket.</u> Not yet published.

Volume 23-25. Doskočilova, M. PLZEŇSKO. Incomplete edition in 1952. Only volume 23 in the GL. County of Plzeň.

Volume 26. Hradecký, E. PODBRDSKO. Printed in 1952. County of Podbrdy.

Volume 27-29. Haas, A. PRACHEŇSKO. Issued 1954; not complete.

Volume 30. Rakovnícko. <u>County Rakovník.</u> Not yet published.

Volume 31. Lísa, Eva. VLTAVSKO. 1951. Vltavský county.

Volume 32. Lišková, M. ŽATECKO. Printed in 1954. Zatec county.

Volume 33. <u>Kladsko</u>. Not yet published.

Volume 34. <u>Slansko.</u> Not published; the original lost. Slaný county.

Pozemkové Knihy (Land Books)

Sometimes called Gruntovní Knihy ("grunt" in old Czech means "family property") or, in the sixteenth and seventeenth centuries, "Purkrechtní Knihy." The Pozemkové Knihy, with the exception of the <u>matriky</u>, are the single most important sources for genealogical research. In many instances the Pozemkové Knihy provide exact family relationships.

The old Pozemkové Knihy originated about the same time as the Patrimoniální Knihy. The term "old" indicates that they are no longer in use. These books are considered public records and are available to anyone for research. At the present time the old books are deposited in the Oblastní Archívy and therefore, automatically become a part of any genealogical search. The oldest Pozemkové Knihy listed the location of the farm or city property, together with the financial obligation of the owner toward the estate owner. Often this obligation consisted of commodities such as chickens, cattle, or hay, rather than actual money. This partially explains why the old Pozemkové Knihy are difficult to locate, for the researcher must establish the name of the estate to which his ancestors' property belonged. For this he would need the aid of a well-informed archivist.

No entry was allowed to be made in the books without the approval of the lord of the country estate or of the city council in urban areas. The books before 1770 list descriptions of the property, while after 1770 they list the old or new conscription numbers (see section on matriky earlier in this chapter). Thus a study of the records of a certain piece of property can give the sequence of generations of the family surname, as ownership was often passed from father to son.

There are numerous other sources helpful in genealogical research; however, most of them are hard to locate or are inaccessible. Again, it should be stressed that the American researchers would do well to make use of the services of the Czechoslovakian Embassy in Washington, D.C. With the knowledge of sources outlined in this chapter, the researcher can make specific requests to the officials at the embassy which will greatly aid them in providing you with a satisfactory and informative reply.

SAMPLES TAKEN FROM THE REPORT OF OBLASTNÍ ARCHÍV IN PLZEŇ

These samples are excellent examples of entries that can be found in the records of vital statistics and matriky in Czechoslovakia. Also they are a tribute to the fine research done by the officials of the archives in Czechoslovakia for American patrons. All entries refer to one family lineage.

1876: The following was found in the birth register of the City National Committee, Book VIII, page 122:

Date of birth: 4 October 1876

Place of birth: Kdyně 200 (New Kdyně)

Full name of the child: Kateřina (Františka) Holubová

Sex: Female

Father: Vojtěch Holub, weaver, Kdyně 200, lawful son
of Václav Holub, citizen of Kdyně No. 117
and his wife, Barbora, born Kwětonová of
Kdyně No. 115.

Mother: Terezie, lawful daughter of Matěj Osvald,
citizen of Kdyně No. 161, and his wife,
Tekla, born Matějovicová from Oprechtice.

Date of christening: 5 May 1877

Church: Catholic

Origin: Legitimate

Midwife: Albína Šimánková, accredited

Godmother: Kateřina Holubová, spinster daughter of
the miller of Kdyně No. 38.

The marriage certificate of the parish of Rechenfelt
by Vienna, of 28 December 1869, was presented.

1835: The following was found in the register of the Catholic church in Kdyně, No. 9, p.249:

Date of the birth and christening: 27 July 1835
Place: House No. 107
Name of the christened: Adalbert Hollub
Religion: Catholic
Sex: Male
Origin: Legitimate
Father: Wenzl Hollub, citizen of here
Mother: Barbara, lawful daughter of Franz Queten,
      citizen of No. 105 and his wife, Josepha, born
      Skokan, of No. 36.
Godparents: Franz Braun, citizen of here and his wife,
      Katharina
Name of the priest: Jacob Faster, chaplain
Midwife: Anna Holub

1788: The following was found in the marriage register of
the Catholic parish in Kdyně, No. 7, page 3:

Date: 12 October 1788
Place: Neugedein 100
Bridegroom: Anton Holub, miller and citizen of No. 100.
Religion: Catholic
Age: 44
Status: Widower
Bride: Anna, daughter of Georg Kohaut, citizen of
      here, No. 102.
Religion: Catholic

Age: 21
Status: Spinster
Witnesses: Jirzi Skokan, citizen of here, Johann
    Impfaul, citizen of here
Priest: Bernard Petirka, deacon

1745: The following was found in the register of the
Catholic church in Kdýně, No. 4, p. 17 (Translated from
Latin):

13 June 1745 was born and baptized Antonius, son of
    Johannes Holub and Anna Maria.
Witnesses: Thoma Imasil, Joanne Schieber of New Kdýně,
    Rosina Imseilin and Anna Mirczin and Adamo
    Schieber of Podzamczi.

In viewing these documents, American genealogists should
consider that the researcher must read through entries in
three different languages. The first entry (1876) is in
Czech, the second and third entries (1835, 1788) are in
German, and the last entry (1745) is in Latin. The multi-
language usage also alters the place names. For example,
the Czech place name Nová Kdýně has been Germanized to
Neugedein. The researcher must also be aware that language
changes affect both given names and surnames. It is important to study the list of given names, included in the
chapter on names. In our samples, the first entry includes
the given names Vojtěch and Václav, which in following
entries have been changed to Adalbert and Wenzl. The
unsuspecting reader might not realize that these are the
same names without having checked the list of given names
(which are arranged alphabetically according to their
Czech version).

In the case of surnames, the first entry gives the correct
Czech spellings, including their female versions, while the
following entries list Germanized versions. So Květen
becomes Queten, Holub becomes Hollub and Rosina Imasilová
becomes Rosina Imseilin, and so forth.

BIBLIOGRAPHY

General

Čapek, Jiří. "Rodopisné prameny v Archívu hlavního města
Prahy." ČASOPIS RODOPISNÉ SPOLEČNOSTI ČESKOSLOVENSKÉ V
PRAZE 14 (1942): 49. In Czech.

Genealogical sources in the archive of the city of
Prague.

Horníček, Ignác. KNIHA O RODOPISU. Prague: n.p., n.d. GL
929.1437 B784e. In Czech.

Analysis of genealogical research.

Krofta, Kamil. DĚJINY SELSKÉHO STAVU. 2d ed. Prague, 1949. In Czech.

> History of peasantry. Valuable for the information given on their customs, mobility, and record keeping.

Markus, Antonin. RODINÁ KRONIKA [Family chronicle]. Populární Úvod do Studia Rodopisného. Prague: Československá akciová tiskárna, 1926. In Czech.

> Popular introduction to genealogical study.

Ottersen, Winston. NOTES ON GENEALOGICAL SOURCES IN BOHEMIA AND MORAVIA. Not available to the public.

> Report on a trip taken to Czechoslovakia by Ottersen himself in 1971 for the purpose of genealogical research. Filed at the Genealogical Library.

Winter, Zikmund. DĚJINY ŘEMESEL A OBCHODU V ČECHÁCH V XIV. A XV. STOLETÍ [History of crafts and commerce in Bohemia in the fourteenth and fifteenth centuries]. Prague, 1906. In Czech.

> Shows routes of caravans bringing merchandise into Bohemia.

Religions

DĚJINY KŘESŤANSTVÍ V ČESKOSLOVENSKU [The history of Christianity in Czechoslovakia]. 6 vols. Prague: 1947-50. In Czech.

> The only complete history of the various churches: Orthodox, Catholic, Hussite, Lutheran, and Bohemian Brethren to 1576. Well documented.

THE JEWS OF CZECHOSLOVAKIA. Historical Studies and Surveys. Philadelphia: The Jewish Publication Society of America, 1968. GL 943.7 F2j.

Zeman, Harold Knox. THE ANABAPTISTS AND THE CZECH BRETHREN IN MORAVIA, 1526-1628. The Hague: Mouton, 1969. GL 943.7 K2a.

> A study of origin and contacts.

Census Records

Dvořaček, František. SOUPISY OBYVATELSTVA V ČECHÁCH, NA MORAVĚ A VE SLEZSKU, V LÉTECH 1754-1921 [Census returns for Bohemia, Moravia and Silesia, 1754-1921]. Vols. 5-7. Prague: Československý statistický věstník 1924-26. In Czech.

Gurtler, Alfred. DIE VOLKSZAHLUNGEN MARIA THERESIAS UND JOSEPH II, 1753-90 [Census returns from the reigns of Maria Theresia and Joseph II, 1753-90]. Innsbruck, Austria: Wagnerische University Buchhandlung, 1909. In German.

Kryl, Rudolf. "Neznámé prameny sčítání obyvatelstva v Čechach." DEMOGRAFIE, REVUE FOR POPULATION RESEARCH, (1961), 253. In Czech.

> Lists little-known sources for population schedules in Bohemia.

MAJOR SOURCES FOR GENEALOGICAL RESEARCH IN CZECHOSLOVAKIA. Salt Lake City: Genealogical Library, in preparation.

Placht, Otto. LIDNATOST A SPOLEČENSKÁ SKLADBA ČESKÉHO STÁTU V 16.-18. STOLETÍ. Prague: Československá akademie věd a umění, 1957. GL 943.7 H6p or microfilm 896,930 (1st item). In Czech.

> Population density and social structure of the Czech lands in the sixteenth and eighteenth centuries.

Šebesta, Edward. POPIS OBYVATELSTVA HLAVNÍHO MĚSTA PRAHY Z ROKU 1770, I - STARÉ MĚSTO. No. 4. Prague: Knihovna Rodopisné společnosti československé, 1933. GL 943.715 x 2p. In Czech.

> Census of the population of the capital city of Prague, 1770. I--Old City.

Land Records

ČESKÉ KATASTRY, 1654-1789. 2d ed. Prague: 1943. In Czech.

> Bohemian cataster books. Analytical study of the land surveys in Bohemia and of peasant conditions in general.

Chalupa, Aleš, comp. TEREZIÁNSKÝ KATASTR ČESKÝ. Vol. 2 and 3. Prague, Archívní správa ministerstva vnitra, 1964. Part of the collection of tax cataster of Bohemia, Moravia, and Silesia, 1957. GL 943.7Be. In Czech.

Dvořáček, František. MORAVSKÉ ZEMSKÉ DESKY, 1480-1683, KRAJ OLOMOUCKÝ. Brno: Zemská banka pro Moravu a Slezsko, 1948-53. GL 943.72 R2m. In Czech.

> Moravian land tablets.

Dvořák, Frantisek. POZEMKOVÁ KNIHA. Prague: Svaz československých soudních úředníků, 1932. In Czech.

> Analysis of the land books published by the Society of the Court clerks. It should be very authentic.

Elznic, Václav. "Původní Mapy Katastrální a Indikační Skyci" [original catastral·maps]. LISTY, no. 14, p.2. In Czech.

Emler, Josef. DESET URBÁŘŮ ČESKÝCH Z DOBY PŘED VÁLKAMI HUSITSKYMI. Prague: Královská česká společnost nauk, 1881. GL 943.71 R2e. In Czech.

Ten tax books from the time prior to the Hussite wars.

Hrubý, František. MORAVSKÉ ZEMSKÉ DESKY Z LET 1348-1642. GL Q 943.72 R2h. In Czech.

Description and sketches of the early land records of Moravia, 1348-1642.

Krejčík, Rudolf Lud, comp. URBÁŘ Z ROKU 1378 A ÚČTY KLÁŠTERA TŘEBOŇSKÉHO Z LET 1367-1407. Prague: Česká akademie věd a umění, 1949. GL 943.717/Tl R2k. In Czech.

Tax book from 1378 and dues paid by citizens to the Třeboň monastery from 1367-1407.

Nový, R., comp. NEJSTARŠÍ ČESKÝ URBÁŘ Z LET 1283-84. Prague: n.p., 1960. In Czech.

Oldest Czech tax books, 1283-84.

Pekař, Josef, comp. ČESKÉ KATASTRY, 1654-1789 [Bohemian tax books, 1654-1789]. Prague: Historický klub, 1932. GL 943.71 R4p. In Czech.

Radímský, Jiří, comp. TEREZIANSKÝ KATASTR MORAVSKÝ. In Prague: Archívní správa ministerstva vnitra, 1957. GL 943.7 B4c. In Czech.

Tax catastre books from the second half of the eighteenth century.

Turek, Adolf, comp. SOUPIS URBÁŘŮ OSTRAVSKÉHO KRAJE, XV.-XVIII. STOLETÍ. Opava, Silesia: Slezský studijní ústav, 1954. GL 943.721 K2t or microfilm 496,677 (3d item). In Czech.

List of tax records of Ostrava district from the fifteenth to eighteenth centuries.

Chapter 6

ARCHIVES

Most people think of an archive as a place where public
records or historical documents are placed and preserved.
However, archives, including those in Czechoslovakia, not
only store and preserve such documents, but also classify,
catalogue and offer them to the public for historical, legal, administrative, demographical, economic, and genealogical research.

Archives in Czechoslovakia are classified according to the
material they contain.

> State Archives (Státní Archív) contain records or
> documents pertaining to the history and legal admin-
> istration of the country.

> District Archives (Státní Oblastní Archívy) contain
> records and documents relating to the jurisdiction
> of the district. These are most important for gene-
> alogical research.

> County Archives (Okresní Archívy) contain records and
> documents concerning the jurisdiction of the county.

> City Archives (Městské Archívy) contain records and
> documents connected with the jurisdiction of the city.
> Some of these also contain matriky and are, therefore,
> important for genealogical research.

> Archives of the estates contain records and documents
> of the estates such as the lists of vassals under
> obligation to the lords. Some of these are also
> deposited in the Státní Oblastní Archívy.

> Archives of educational institutions and branches of
> the government, such as the military archives, con-
> tain materials that could be helpful in genealogical
> research, but in most instances, their use is re-
> stricted.

Before the use of these archives is discussed in detail,
it should be stressed that the Czech government does not

encourage the archivists or other employees of these institutions to perform genealogical research. The government
prefers that the foreign researchers utilize the services
of the Czechoslovakian embassies (in the United States the
address is: The Czechoslovakian Embassy, 3900 Linnean Ave.,
N.W., Washington, D.C. 20008). Although local residents
in Czechoslovakia can visit the reading room of the archives,
request the use of certain books for a small fee, and copy
the data, the Czech law specifies that each visitor can
work only on his own ancestry. Even though this law is
not always enforced, anyone caught not respecting it may be
barred from the use of the archives altogether. Above all,
Czech citizens are not allowed to mail abroad material
copied from the archival books. Do not make requests of
family, friends, acquaintances or employees of the archives
to copy records, as it places them in a very difficult
position. Remember also, that this work, done on the sly,
is often subject to error. It would, of course, be desir-
able if we could do research directly in the archives or
other record depositories in Czechoslovakia itself, but
since the Czechoslovakian authorities have presently decided otherwise, it is necessary to comply with their desires.

All of the aforementioned archives publish brochures or
books listing their complete holdings. Some few years ago
the Genealogical Library of the Latter-Day Saints Church
was fortunate enough to purchase these archival guides. Of
course, they are written in Czech, with some prefaces written in German or Russian. A list of all the Czech archival
guides on file at the Genealogical Library is given in the
bibliography which follows this chapter.

Although at the present time no actual genealogical research
in Czechoslovakian records can be performed here in America,
much preparatory work can be accomplished with the proper
use of the tools that are found in the library. In the
chapter "Czech and Slovak Immigration to America," the
groundwork has been laid for obtaining the name of the
birthplace of an individual's Czechoslovakian ancestors.
The next step is to establish the county where this place
is located. This can be done with the help of the GE-
MEINDELEXIKON, which is also on file at the Genealogical
Library. This lexicon lists the places in Czech, with
equivalents in Hungarian and German. The index is excellent; but the sequence of the alphabet is according to the
Czech order, so one must study the section on the Czech
and Slovak alphabets.

The present administrative units in Czechoslovakia are not
counties, but oblasti (districts). The oblast is the official designation for district, but the term kraj is sometimes used. Each district includes several former counties.
The archives are also divided by oblast or district. To
help the reader better understand this administrative
division, a map showing the outlines of these districts is
included. An alphabetical listing of the counties, showing the district in which they are now located, has also
been included here.

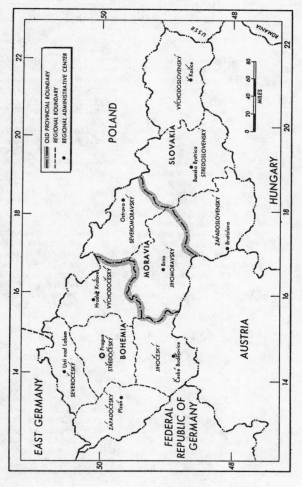

Archival Districts (Political Subdivisions)

ZEME CESKE (BOHEMIA, MORAVIA, SILESIA)

County	Czech name of the Kraj	English name of the District
Benešov	Středočeský Kraj	Central Bohemian District
Beroun	Středočeský Kraj	Central Bohemian District
Blansko	Jihomoravský Kraj	South Moravian District
Brno Město	Jihomoravsky Kraj	South Moravian District
Brno Venkov	Jihomoravsky Kraj	South Moravian District
Bruntál	Severomoravský Kraj	North Moravian District
Břeclav	Jihomoravský Kraj	South Moravian District
Česká Lípa	Severočeský Kraj	North Bohemian District
České Budějovice	Jihočeský Kraj	South Bohemian District
Český Krumlov	Jihočeský Kraj	South Bohemian District
Děčín	Severočeský Kraj	North Bohemian District
Domažlice	Západočeský Kraj	West Bohemian District
Frýdek	Severomoravský Kraj	North Moravian District
Gottwaldov	Jihomoravský Kraj	South Moravian District
Havlíčkuv Brod	Západočeský Kraj	West Bohemian District
Hodonín	Jihomoravský Kraj	South Moravian District
Hradec Králové	Východočeský Kraj	East Bohemian District
Cheb	Západočeský Kraj	West Bohemian District
Chomutov	Severočeský Kraj	North Bohemian District
Chrudim	Východočeský Kraj	East Bohemian District
Jablonec n/Nisou	Severočeský Kraj	North Bohemian District
Jičín	Východočeský Kraj	East Bohemian District
Jihlava	Jihomoravský Kraj	South Moravian District
Jindřichův Hradec	Jihočeský Kraj	South Bohemian District
Karlovy Vary	Západočeský Kraj	West Bohemian District
Karviná	Severomoravský Kraj	North Bohemian District
Kladno	Středočeský Kraj	Central Bohemian District
Klatovy	Západočeský Kraj	West Bohemian District
Kolín	Středočeský Kraj	Central Bohemian District
Kroměříž	Jihomoravský Kraj	South Moravian District
Kutná Hora	Středočeský Kraj	Central Bohemian District
Liberec	Severočeský Kraj	North Bohemian District
Litoměřice	Severočeský Kraj	North Bohemian District
Louny	Severočeský Kraj	North Bohemian District
Mělník	Stredočeský Kraj	Central Bohemian District
Mladá Boleslav	Středočeský Kraj	Central Bohemian District
Most	Severočeský Kraj	North Bohemian District
Náchod	Východočeský Kraj	East Bohemian District
Nový Jičín	Severomoravský Kraj	North Moravian District

County	Czech name of the Kraj	English name of the District
Nymburk	Středočeský Kraj	Central Bohemian District
Olomouc	Severomoravský Kraj	North Moravian District
Opava	Severomoravský Kraj	North Moravian District
Pardubice	Východočeský Kraj	East Bohemian District
Pelhřimov	Jihočeský Kraj	South Bohemian District
Písek	Jihočeský Kraj	South Bohemian District
Plzeň Sever (North)	Západočeský Kraj	West Bohemian District
Plzeň Jih (South)	Západočeský Kraj	West Bohemian District
Prachatice	Jihočeský Kraj	South Bohemian District
Praha Východ (East)	Středočeský Kraj	Central Bohemian District
Praha Západ (West)	Středočeský Kraj	Central Bohemian District
Přerov	Severomoravský Kraj	North Moravian District
Příbram	Středočeský Kraj	Central Bohemian District
Prostějov	Jihomoravský Kraj	South Moravian District
Rakovník	Středočeský Kraj	Central Bohemian District
Rokycany	Západočeský Kraj	West Bohemian District
Rychnov n/Kněžnou	Východočeský Kraj	East Bohemian District
Semily	Východočeský Kraj	East Bohemian District
Strakonice	Jihočeský Kraj	South Bohemian District
Sokolov	Západočeský Kraj	West Bohemian District
Svitavy	Východočeský Kraj	East Bohemian District
Šumperk	Severomoravský Kraj	North Moravian District
Tábor	Jihočeský Kraj	South Bohemian District
Tachov	Západočeský Kraj	West Bohemian District
Teplice	Severočeský Kraj	North Bohemian District
Trutnov	Východočeský Kraj	East Bohemian District
Třebíč	Jihomoravský Kraj	South Moravian District
Uherské Hradiště	Jihomoravský Kraj	South Moravian District
Ústí n/Labem	Severočeský Kraj	North Bohemian District
Ústí n/Orlicí	Východočeský Kraj	East Bohemian District
Všetin	Severomoravský Kraj	North Moravian District
Vyškov	Jihomoravský Kraj	South Moravian District
Znojmo	Jihomoravský Kraj	South Moravian District
Žďár n/Sázavou	Jihomoravský Kraj	South Moravian District

SLOVAKIA

County	Czech name of the kraj	English name of the District
Báňa Nová	Západoslovenský Kraj	West Slovakian District

County	Czech name of the kraj	English name of the District
Bánovce n/Bebra-vou	Západoslovenský Kraj	West Slovakian District

Parish registers are in the Nitra Branch

County	Czech name of the kraj	English name of the District
Bardějov	Východoslovenský Kraj	East Slovakian District
Bátovce	Západoslovenský Kraj	West Slovakian District

Matriky deposited in the Nitra Branch

County	Czech name of the kraj	English name of the District
Bratislava Venkov	Západoslovenský Kraj	West Slovakian District
Bratislavá Mesto	Zapadoslovenský Kraj	West Slovakian District
Bystrica Bánská	Středoslovenský Kraj	Middle Slovakian District
Bystrica Povážska	Středoslovenský Kraj	Middle Slovakian District
Bytča	Středoslovenský Kraj	Middle Slovakian District

Matriky deposited in the Bytca District

County	Czech name of the kraj	English name of the District
Cajakovo	Západoslovenský Kraj	West Slovakian District
Calovo	Západoslovenský Kraj	West Slovakian District
Dvory n/Žitavou	Západoslovenský Kraj	West Slovakian District

Matriky deposited in the Nitra Branch

County	Czech name of the kraj	English name of the District
Feledince	Středoslovenský Kraj	Middle Slovakian District
Galanta	Západoslovenský Kraj	West Slovakian District
Gelnica	Východoslovenský Kraj	East Slovakian District

Matriky deposited in the Kosice District

County	Czech name of the kraj	English name of the District
Giraltovce	Východoslovenský Kraj	East Slovakian District
Hlohovec	Západoslovenský Kraj	West Slovakian District

Matriky deposited in the Nitra Branch

County	Czech name of the kraj	English name of the District
Hrádok Liptovský	Středoslovenský Kraj	Middle Slovakian District

Matriky deposited in the Bytča Branch

County	Czech name of the kraj	English name of the District
Humenné	Východoslovenský kraj	East Slovakian District
Ilava	Stredoslovenský Kraj	Middle Slovakian District

Matriky deposited in the Bytca Branch

Kámeň Modrý	Stredoslovenský Kraj	Middle Slovakian District
Kapušany Velké	Východoslovenský Kraj	East Slovakian District
Kežmarok	Východoslovenský Kraj	East Slovakian District

Matriky deposited in the Kosice Branch

Komárno	Západoslovenský Kraj	West Slovakian District

Matriky deposited in the Kosice Branch

Košice Mesto	Východoslovenský Kraj	East Slovakian District
Košice Venkov	Východoslovenský Kraj	East Slovakian District
Kremnica	Stredoslovenský Kraj	Middle Slovakian District

Matriky deposited in the Bytca Branch

Krupiná	Stredoslovenský Kraj	Middle Slovakian District

Matriky deposited in the Bytca Branch

Kubín Dolní	Stredoslovenský Kraj	Middle Slovakian District

Matriky deposited in the Bytca Branch

Kysucké Nové Mesto	Stredoslovenský Kraj	Middle Slovakian District

Matriky deposited in the Bytca Branch

Levice	Západoslovenský Kraj	West Slovakian Dictrict

Matriky deposited in the Nitra Branch

Levoča	Východoslovenský Kraj	East Slovakian District

Matriky deposited in the Kosice Branch

County	Czech name of the kraj	English name of the District
Lubovňa Stará	Východoslovenský Kraj	East Slovakian District
Lučenec	Středoslovenský Kraj	Middle Slovakian District
Malacky	Západoslovenský Kraj	West Slovakian District
Martin Turčiansky Svatý	Středoslovenský Kraj	Middle Slovakian District

Matriky deposited in the Bytca Branch

Modra	Středoslovenský Kraj	Middle Slovakian District

Matriky deposited in the Bytca Branch

Mojmírovce	Západoslovenský Kraj	Western Slovakian District
Moldava n/Bodvrou	Východoslovenský Kraj	East Slovakian District

Matriky deposited in the Kosice Branch

Moravce Zlaté	Středoslovenský Kraj	Middle Slovakian District
Myjava	Západoslovenský Kraj	West Slovakian District
Námestové	Středoslovenský Kraj	Middle Slovakian District

Matriky deposited in the Bytca Branch

Nitra	Západoslovenský Kraj	West Slovakian District

Matriky deposited in the Nitra Branch

Parkan	Středoslovenský Kraj	Middle Slovakian District
Pezinok	Západoslovenský Kraj	West Slovakian District
Pieštany	Západoslovenský Kraj	West Slovakian District
Poprad	Východoslovenský Kraj	East Slovakian District

Matriky deposited in the Kosice Branch

Preselany	Západoslovenský Kraj	West Slovakian District

Matriky deposited in the Nitra Branch

County	Czech name of the kraj	English name of the District
Prievidze	Západoslovenský Kraj	West Slovakian District
	Matriky deposited in the Nitra Branch	
Púchov	Stredoslovenský Kraj	Middle Slovakian District
	Matriky deposited in the Bytca Branch	
Radošina	Západoslovenský Kraj	West Slovakian District
	Matriky deposited in the Nitra Branch	
Rajec	Stredoslovenský Kraj	Middle Slovakian District
	Matriky deposited in the Bytca Branch	
Rožnava	Východoslovenský Kraj	East Slovakian District
	Matriky deposited in the Kosice Branch	
Ružomberok	Stredoslovenský Kraj	Middle Slovakian District
	Matriky deposited in the Bytca Branch	
Sabinov	Východoslovenský Kraj	East Slovakian District
Salka	Západoslovenský Kraj	West Slovakian District
	Matriky deposited in the Nitra Branch	
Sečovce	Východoslovenský Kraj	East Slovakian District
	Matriky deposited in the Kosice Branch	
Senec	Západoslovenský Kraj	West Slovakian District
Senica	Západoslovenský Kraj	West Slovakian District
Sered	Západoslovenský Kraj	West Slovakian District
Skalica	Západoslovenský Kraj	West Slovakian District
Snina	Východoslovenský Kraj	East Slovakian District
Sobota Rimavská	Východoslovenský Kraj	East Slovakian District
Sobrance	Východoslovenský Kraj	East Slovakian District

County	Czech name of the kraj	English name of the District
Spišská Nová Ves	Východoslovenský Kraj	East Slovakian District
Streda Dunajská	Západoslovenský Kraj	West Slovakian District
Stropkov	Východoslovenský Kraj	East Slovakian District
Samorin	Západoslovenský Kraj	West Slovakian District
Štiavnica Bánská	Západoslovenský Kraj	West Slovakian District

Matriky deposited in the Nitra Branch

Tornala	Stredoslovenský Kraj	Middle Slovakian District

Matriky deposited in the Bytca Branch

Trenčín	Západoslovenský Kraj	West Slovakian District
Trnava	Západoslovenský Kraj	West Slovakian District

Matriky deposited in the Nitra Branch

Trstená	Stredoslovenský Kraj	Middle Slovakian District

Matriky deposited in the Bytca Branch

Turčianske Teplice	Stredoslovenský Kraj	Middle Slovakian District

Matriky deposited in the Bytca Branch

Velké Koštalany	Západoslovenský Kraj	West Slovakian District

Matriky deposited in the Nitra Branch

Velké Záluzie	Západoslovenský Kraj	West Slovakian District

Matriky deposited in the Nitra Branch

Velký Cetín	Západoslovenský Kraj	West Slovakian District

Matriky deposited in the Nitra Branch

Velké Kapušany	Východoslovenský Kraj	East Slovakian District

County	Czech name of the kraj	English name of the District
Ves Spišska Nová	Středoslovenský Kraj	Middle Slovakian District
	Matriky deposited in the Bytca Branch	
Ves Spišská Stará	Středoslovenský Kraj	Middle Slovakian District
	Matriky deposited in the Bytca Branch	
Vráble	Západoslovenský Kraj	West Slovakian District
	Matriky deposited in the Nitra Branch	
Vranov n/Toplou	Východoslovenský Kraj	East Slovakian District
Zámky Nové	Západoslovenský Kraj	West Slovakian District
	Matriky deposited in the Nitra Branch	
Zlaté Moravce	Západoslovenský Kraj	West Slovakian District
	Matriky deposited in the Nitra Branch	
Zvoleň	Středoslovenský Kraj	Middle Slovakian District
Želiezovce	Západoslovenský Kraj	West Slovakian District
	Matriky deposited in the Nitra Branch	
Žilina	Středoslovenský Kraj	Middle Slovakian District
	Matriky deposited in the Bytca Branch	

Now that the researcher knows the name of the ancestral residence in Czechoslovakia, the county (župa in the Slovakian language) in which it is situated, and the name of the archive under whose jurisdiction the county falls, he is ready to use the archival guides in the Genealogical Library. It has been mentioned before that, with very few exceptions, all the matriky up to 1869 have been deposited in the Státní Oblastní Archívy (Státný Archív in Slovakia).

The counties in the district are listed in the particular archival guide in their alphabetical order, and in turn the parishes in each county follow in their alphabetical order. The following is a sample of the information as found in the archival guide of the South Bohemian District, followed by the English translation:

OKRES JINDŘICHŮV HRADEC

1/ Jindřichův Hradec.
M.o. Jindřichův Hradec.
Kolem r. 1256 dal Oldřich I. z Hradce patronální právo nad farou v Jindř. Hradci řádu německých rytířů a od té doby ji spravovali. Po odchodu členů řádu nebyla fara spravována. Katolický farář se uvádí až k r.1483. R. 1625 povýšil papež Urban VIII. faru na proboštství. Má 47 matrik z let 1700-1869, a 6 indexů. F.o.: Buk, Děbolín, Dolní Skrýchov, Dolní Žďár, Drahýška, Horní Lhota, Horní Žďár, Jindřichův Hradec, Jindřiš, Matná, Otín, Radounka.
Matriky: n. 1705-1867
         o. 1700-1861
         z. 1700-1869
Index: 6 knih.

Translation:

COUNTY JINDRICHUV HRADEC

1/Jindřichův Hradec (City)
Jurisdiction of the matriky. Jindřichův Hradec.
Around the year 1256 the king, Oldřich I, gave the jurisdiction over the Hradec parish to the order of German Knights, who has administered it since. After the brethren of the order departed, the parish was without the leadership. First mention of a Catholic priest appears in 1483. In 1625 the pope, Urban VIII, bestowed the rank of presbytery to the parish. There are 47 matriky covering the years 1700-1869 and 6 books of indexes. The jurisdiction of the parish: Buk, Děbolín, Dolní Skrýchov, Dolní Žďár, Drahýška, Horní Lhota, Horní Žďár, Jindřichův Hradec, Jindřiš, Matná, Otín, Radounka.
Matriky: births 1705-1867
         marriages 1700-1861
         deaths 1700-1869
Indexes: 6 books

Similar information is listed for each parish. In some instances the parish originated later by division from another parish; this is explained in the descriptions of each parish. If, for example, a new parish was formed in 1775, obviously, the records which cover the period prior to 1775 will be found in the matriky of the original parish. This information should make it possible to place an accurate and well-directed research order with the Czechoslovakian Embassy in Washington, D.C.

STÁTNÍ OBLASTNÍ ARCHÍVY (STATE DISTRICT ARCHIVES) IN CZECH LANDS

All the archival guides for the state Oblastní Archívy have been published in Prague, by the Archívní správa minister- stva vnitra (archival department of the Ministery of Inter- ior). They are parts of the Průvodce po archívních fondech. (GL 943.7 A5sa)

JIHOČESKÝ KRAJ. Vols. 8-11. 1957-59.

> Archive is situated in Třeboň, Bohemia. Volume 8 contains a list of parishes.

JIHOMORAVSKÝ KRAJ. Vols. 1, 17 and 20. 1954-64.

> Situated in Brno, Moravia. Matriky are deposited in the MĚSTSKY ARCHÍV (City Archives), Brno. GL 943.7 A 5sa.

SEVEROČESKÝ KRAJ. Vol. 9 and 16. 1959-63.

> Situated in Litoměřice, Bohemia. Volume 9 contains a list of parishes.

SEVEROMORAVSKÝ KRAJ. Vols. 5, 12 and 15. 1957, 1961 and 1969.

> Situated in Opava, Silesia. Volume 5 contains a list of parishes.

STREDOČESKÝ KRAJ. Vol. 6 and 13. 1958-60.

> Situated in the city of Prague. Volume 6 contains a list of parishes outside of the city of Prague. The list of parishes in the city of Prague has been pub- lished in a separate brochure: Hlavsa, Václav. PRAŽSKÉ MATRIKY FARNÍ, 1584-1870. Prague: Archív hlavního města Prahy, 1954. GL 943.7 Al No. 8 or microfilm 908,084 (item 2).

VÝCHODOČESKÝ KRAJ. Vols. 18-19. 1965.

> Situated in Zámrsk, Bohemia. Both contain a list of parishes.

ZÁPADOČESKÝ KRAJ. Vol. 7. 1958.

> Situated in Pilsen, Bohemia. Volume 7 contains a list of parishes.

STÁTNE ARCHÍVY (STATE ARCHIVES) IN SLOVAKIA

All Slovakian archival guides were published by Slovenská Archívná správa in Bratislava and are parts of series Sprievodca po archívnych fondoch. GL 943.7 A5sas.

STREDOSLOVENSKÝ KRAJ. Vols. 5 and 13. 1962 and 1969.

    Situated in Bánská Bystrica. Volume 5 contains a list
of parishes. A branch of Státný Archív in Banska
Bystrica is situated in Bytča, Slovakia. Volume 2
(1959) contains a list of parishes.

VÝCHODOSLOVENSKÝ KRAJ. Vol. 3, 4, and 10. 1963 and 1965.

    Situated in Prešov. Volume 2 contains a list of
parishes. Branch of Státný Archív Prešov is situated in Košice. Volume 10 contains a list of parishes.

ZÁPADOSLOVENSKÝ KRAJ. Vols. 1, 7, 8, 9, and 12. 1959 and
1964.

    Situated in Bratislava. Volume 1 contains a list of
parishes.

    A branch of Státný Archív Bratislava is in Nitra.
Volume 6 contains a list of parishes.

BIBLIOGRAPHY

This bibliography begins with general publications concerning the archives in Czechoslovakia, followed by the publications referring to specific types of archives as outlined
in the foregoing text of this chapter. For publications
among the holdings of the Genealogical Library, the call
numbers have been provided. Of the libraries in the United
States, the Genealogical Library has in its files the largest collection of genealogical aids for research on Czechoslovakian ancestry. There is much additional literature in
Czechoslovakia itself; and perhaps at some future date this
too will be added to the collection of the Genealogical
Library.

ARCHÍVNÍ ČASOPIS. Prague: Archívní správa ministerstva
vnitra. GL 943.7 B2a. (The Genealogical Library has only
the 1951 issue.)

    Periodical of the Czechoslovak archives, published
by the archival department of the Ministery of
Interior.

ARCHÍVNÍ PUBLIKACE. Prague: Archívní správa ministerstva
vnitra, 1965. GL 943.7 Al No 7 or microfilm 896,839 (8th
item).

    Bibliography of the publications of the Czechoslova-
kian archives.

Bauer, Otakar. SOUPIS ARCHÍVNÍ LITERATŮRY V ČESKÝCH ZEMÍCH,
1895-1956. Prague: Archívní správa ministerstva vnitra,
1959. GL 943.7 A3b.

    Bibliography of archival publications for the České
Země, 1895-1956.

Holl, Ivo, et al. PRŮVODCE PO ARCHÍVNÍCH FONDECH. Vol. 6.
Prague: Archívní správa ministerstva vnitra, 1958. GL
943.7 A5sa.

A guide to the archival collections.

SBORNÍK ARCHÍVNÍCH PRÁCÍ. Prague: Archívní správa ministerstva vnitra, 1970. GL 943.7 B4sb no 2.

Bibliography of works on archives.

SLOVENSKÁ ARCHIVISTIKA. Bratislava: Slovenská archívna
správa. GL 943.7 B2s. (Genealogical Library has only 1955
issue).

Periodical of the Slovakian archives.

State Archives

STÁTNÍ ÚSTŘEDNÍ ÚSTAV V PRAZE. Vol. 2. Průvodce po archívních fondech series. Prague: Archívní správa ministerstva
vnitra, 1955. GL 943.7 A5sa.

Holdings of the state central archives in Prague.

County Archives

The following is a list of county and city archives. Most
of the counties prior to 1949 and cities created their own
archives, independent of the State District Archives, and
published their own guides. If these guides have been purchased by the Genealogical Library, the call numbers will
be given. The arrangement of the items is in alphabetical
order by place rather than by author.

Skutil, Jan. OKRESNÍ ARCHÍV V BLANSKU. Moravia: Okresní
archív v Blansku, n.d.

County archives for the city of Blansko, Moravia.

OKRESNÍ A MĚSTSKÝ ARCHÍV V ČESKÉM BRODĚ, MĚSTSKÝ ARCHÍV V
KOSTELCI n/ČERNÝMI LESY. Ceský Brod: County archives, 1959.

City and county archives for Ceský Brod; city archives
for Kostelec n/Černými Lesy, Bohemia.

Srch, Eduard. OKRESNÍ ARCHÍV V ČESKÉM KRUMLOVĚ. Český
Krumlov, Okresní národní výbor, 1958. GL 943.7 A50.

County archives for Český Krumlov, Bohemia.

Kajdoš, Vladimír. OKRESNÍ ARCHÍV VE FRENŠTÁTĚ POD RADHOŠTĚM.
Frenštát pod Radhoštěm: Okresní národní výbor, 1959.

County archives for Frenštát pod Radhoštěm, Moravia.

OKRESNÍ ARCHÍV V JINDŘICHOVĚ HRADCI. Vol. 6. Jindřichův Hradec: Okresní národní výbor, 1959. GL 943.7 A5ar.

County archives for Jindřichův Hradec, Bohemia.

OKRESNÍ A MĚSTSKÝ ARCHÍV V KOLÍNĚ. Vol. 4. Kolín: Okresní archív, 1961. GL 943.7 A5po.

County and city archives for Kolín, Bohemia.

Luzek, Bořivoj. OKRESNÍ ARCHÍV V LOUNECH. Prague: n.p., 1958.

County archives for Louny, Bohemia.

Sedláková, M. OKRESNÍ ARCHÍV V MILEVSKU. Vol. 2. Písek: Okresní archív, 1958. GL 943.7 A5ar.

County archives for Milevsko, Bohemia.

OKRESNÍ ARCHÍV V MLADÉ BOLESLAVI. Vol. 2. Mladá Boleslav: Krajský národní výbor, 1958. GL 943.7 A5po.

County archives for Mladá Boleslav, Bohemia. Contains also the city archives for Benátky n/Jizerou, Kosmonosy and Dobrovice.

OKRESNÍ ARCHÍV PRAHA-ZÁPAD. Vol. 5. Prague: Okresní archív, 1964. GL 943.7 A5po.

County archives for Prague-West.

OKRESNÍ ARCHÍV V SOBĚSLAVI. Soběslav, 1958.

County archives for Soběslav, Bohemia.

OKRESNÍ ARCHÍV V TÁBOŘE. Tábor, 1958.

County archives for Tábor, Bohemia.

City Archives

Vojtíšek, Václav. O ARCHÍVECH MĚSTSKÝCH A OBECNÍCH A JEJICH SPRÁVĚ. Vol. 2. Prague: Spolek československých knihovníků, 1924.

Discusses the city archives and their administration. Published by the Organization of the Czechoslovakian Librarians.

Volf, Miloslav. POPIS MĚSTSKÝCH ARCHÍVŮ V ČECHÁCH. Prague: Zemský národní výbor, 1947. GL 943.71 A5a.

An account of the holdings of the city archives in Bohemia published by the State National Committee.

ARCHÍV MESTA BRATISLAVY. Vol. 1. Bratislava: Archívná správa ministerstva vnutra, 1955. GL 943.7 A5r.

Archives of the city of Bratislava, Slovakia.

ARCHÍV MĚSTA BRNA. Vol. 3. Prague: Archívní správa ministerstva vnitra, 1957. GL 943.7 A5r.

Archives of the city of Brno, Moravia.

ARCHÍV MESTA KOŠIC. Vol. 5. Prague: Archívní správa ministerstva vnitra, 1957. GL 943.7 A5r.

Archives of the city of Košice, Slovakia.

ARCHÍV MESTA KREMNICE, Vol. 7. Bratislava: Slovenská archívná správa poverenictva vnutra, 1957. GL 943.7 A5r.

Archives of the city of Kremnice, Slovakia.

MĚSTSKÝ ARCHÍV V OSTRAVĚ. Vol. 8. Ostrava: Městský národní výbor, 1967. GL 943.7 A5ar.

Archives of the city of Ostrava, Moravia.

Bělohlávek, Miloslav. PRŮVODCE PO ARCHÍVU PLZEŇ. Pilsen: Městský národní výbor, 1954. GL 943.7 A5ma or microfilm 896,822 (4th item).

Guide to the city archives of Pilsen, Bohemia.

Miscellaneous

Krejčík, Adolf Ludvík. PŘÍSPĚVEK K SOUPISU ARCHÍVŮ VELKÝCH STATKŮ. 2 vols. Prague: Československá akademie zemědělská, 1929.

Contribution to the listing of holdings of the archives of large estates. Published by the Czechoslovak agricultural academy.

Kučera, Karel. ARCHÍV UNIVERSITY KARLOVY. Prague: Karlova universita, 1961. GL 943.7 A5u.

Archives of the Charles University in Prague.

Chapter 7

NAMES

In genealogical research a person's name is one of the most important keys to the past (the others, of course, being dates and places). It is not within the confines of this chapter to include everything that is known about Czech given and surnames, but the reader will be given an idea concerning the origin, possible misspellings or variations (feminine versions) of some common surnames. In addition, some given names will be identified as modern and, therefore, not to be found in the matriky and other old documents.

When the forefather of the Czechs (whose name was Čech) and his company arrived in the center of Bohemia, they were the only settlers there. Each individual was known merely by his given name. Even as the population multiplied and additional settlements were founded, there still was not much need for surnames. Individuals having the same given name were simply identified by a system of patronymics, for example, Bořivoj, Přemyslův syn (Bořivoj, son of Přemysl). This was sufficient for some centuries.

The noble families were the first to assume family names; and, as in the greater part of the Western world, they derived their surnames from their territorial property. Thus we find, for example, names such as Jan z Dubé, Ondřej z Říčan ("z" is an equivalent of French "de," German "von," or English "of"). The advantages and disadvantages of this system are discussed in the chapter on heraldry.

There were many irregularities in the system of patronymics, depending on the skill of the scribe or priest who kept the matriky. As late as the sixteenth century, one can find in the city registers entries such as Václav, syn Janků (Václav, son of the Janeks); Václav's son, in turn, was named Jankovec, and his son, Jan Kovec. It is not known whether this family would then have kept the surname Kovec.

The origin of surnames among the common folk are often based upon customs prevalent in early times. The drivers of the teams of horses or donkeys that pulled the carts bringing salt, wine, spice and also cloth to Bohemia, were called Provodce (Průvodce)--in English "one who accompanies." Their houses were called "u Průvodců"--at the Průvodce, which often remained as a family surname. The farmers felt

themselves superior to the cottagers who did not own as
many fields as the farmers did. As a result, farmers called
them contemptuously "žabaři, plévy, plévkové"--in English
probably "peasants." There are many such surnames, some
going back to the Hussite Wars (1352-1433). The Hussite
followers asked among themselves, "Kak si?" ("How are
you?") which gave rise to the surname, Kaksové. They also
cautioned each other to keep their heads protected by their
shields, "Krej sa," thus the surname Krejsa. The surnames
Nebojsa, Nezlobsa, Vzalroha (he took the corner and ran
away), and Utíkálek (he who runs from the battle) originated from the times of the Hussite wars.

Following the Hussite wars for several hundred years, the
Czechs named their children after the ancient prophets or
apostles providing new sources for surnames: from Adam
came the surname, Adámek; Michal--Michálek; Jan--Jenek,
Janeček, Jeníček, Janda, Jenda, Honzík, and Honzíček.

The empress Maria Theresia in about 1740 issued an order
that surnames be used in addition to given names. Unfortunately many Jews came by their surnames in a very humiliating way (described on p. 43). Other Czech citizens simply
accepted the surnames used in the matriky by the parish ministers when christening children, marrying the couples and
burying the deceased. These surnames had their origins in
the way the people lived, acted, worked, looked, or the description of the places where they lived. Thus, unless the
surname was of foreign origin, it meant something. In the
following few paragraphs, the origins of some of the old
surnames, along with their English equivalents will be discussed.

Names from wars were Turek (Turk), Polák (Pole), Rus (Russian), Němec (German), Švejda (Swede), and Pružák (Prussian).
At the end of the Thirty Years' War in 1620, many families
were exiled or chose to leave the country and their estates
or farmhouses were left vacant. The foreign nobility brought
people from abroad to reinhabit them. Some of the newcomers were dark gypsies, previously unknown in Bohemia.
Their homes and their families were called Cikáni (gypsies),
or Černý (the black one). Other settlers were called Nový,
Novák, Novotný, Nováček, Novotníček--all of them variations
of Newman. Although today these are very common and wide-
spread Czech surnames, prior to the nineteenth century all
people who shared a surname and resided in the same locality
could be considered relatives. This is particularly true
if other conditions are identical such as the given names
of the parents, time given, occupations, and conscription
house number.

Surnames were also based on the character of the original
ancestor: Bezděka (not too smart), Hubáček (talker),
Zubatej or Teplej (of sharp tongue), Nečina (lazy one),
Nedbal (does not care), Všetečka (curious one), and Divoký
(wild one)-- to name only a few. People were not very kind

to their neighbors who had unusual physical features and used these features as a basis for a surname: Hrbec (hunchback), Cvrček (cricket, someone who is very small), Chromý (one who limps), Široký (huge), and Bělohlávek (albino). Surnames also denoted the quality and color of skin and hair: Pěkný (nice), Kudrnáč (of wavy hair), Černý (black), Holec, Holeček (without beard). Property values also gave rise to surnames: Bohatý, Boháč (rich), Chudý (poor), Mizera (destitute). One who indulged in fancy clothes was named Fanfrnoch (clotheshorse, dandy); Hezký meant "nice one" and one who imbibed in spirits, Bíba. (In the Middle Ages Bíba was an expression denoting a toast.) One who was unscrupulous in his business dealings was sure to be named Šebela.

There were people who in their speech used the same favorite expression over and over again; their surnames would have been: Víme (do you know), Hele, Helement (look here), or Sakra (damn). Some surnames tell us that the ancestors of the current bearers of the name loved to dance: Podlaha (floor), Hopsasa, Přetrhdílo (interrupted his work), and Vejkruta (dances around).

Even the days of the week were a source of surnames: Pondělíček (little Monday), Středa, Pátek, Sobotka (Saturday--this was a favorite of the Jews who became Christians). Some surnames originated from religious vocabulary: Říman (Roman), Křížek (little cross), Papež (pope), Farář (minister), Zborník (referring to an organizational unit within the Czech Brethren Church--sbor), Žid (Jew), and Nemodlenec (one who does not pray).

Many people accepted the surnames related to their occupations: Švec (shoemaker), Kadlec (weaver), Petržílek (gardener), Houska (baker), Krejčí (taylor), Kovář (smith), Uhlík or Uhlíř (coalman), Rybák (fisherman). The animal and marine world gave rise to many surnames, such as Jelen (deer), Jelínek (little deer), Kráva (cow), Kozák (goat), Koníček (little horse), Kapr (carp), and Úhoř, Ouhoř, or Ouhora (eel).

The geographical description of the residence of some people also served as sources for very common surnames: Horák, also Horáček (one who lives in the mountains), Dolák (one who lives in a valley), Zadní (one whose property is in the back of another structure), Rybnický (lake), and Klatovský (one who resided in the then small village of Klatovy).

When Emperor Joseph II issued an order that the <u>matriky</u> were to be kept in German or Latin and not in Czech, some priests, resenting the use of German, used Latin and often translated both the Czech given names and surnames directly. This gave rise to such unusual surnames as Ventris (from Bříska--stomach) and Hortensius (for Zahradník--gardener). In addition, many German surnames were translated into Czech and vice versa. So German Wieser became Vyzera, Reich--Rajch, Long--Lonka, Vencl--Fencl; the Czech name Němec turned into Nemethy, and Vojíř into Woyrsch.

These and other changes in surnames may confuse the genealogist unless he is aware of the customs, language, and ini-
tial instability of the surnames. For example, a young man
who married and took over the farm or cottage of his bride's
parents often assumed her family surname as well, and from
then on his progeny were known by that surname. When his
children were christened, the parish clerk or minister might
make a note of this change in the matriky, using the expressions kdysi (formerly) and vulgo (alias). The same situation might arise concerning families that were transferred
by the feudal lords to a better locality, often some dis-
tance away. Thus Kodym, who was transferred to a village
called Machovina, would receive a new surname--Macha. When
a young man learned a trade and became a member of his
guild, he had the privilege of adding the word of his trade
to his father's surname. In another generation the original
surname was dropped and the descendants were known by the
name of his trade. For example, Kecal, who learned the
trade of a blacksmith (kovar) would assume the surname Kovar.

The Czech alphabet became stabilized and "modernized" at the
end of the sixteenth century when the Kralická Bible was
printed. Unfortunately, many scribes and parish ministers
persisted in using the cumbersome, archaic form of the alphabet till about the middle of the nineteenth century. However, with the introduction of the "modern" Czech alphabet,
many names were spelled phonetically and when pronounced
sounded like their original version. In the modern alphabet there is no "w"; and even in the Middle Ages when the
w was still used, it was pronounced simply as "v." One
can find many w's in the matriky as recently as one hundred
years ago. They are to be interpreted as v's. Also, there
are some consonants that appear with a pronunciation mark
"✓" (see the chapter "Language") which means that they are
to be pronounced softly. In archaic Czech and in some modern instances, this soft pronunciation was indicated by a
conglomeration of letters, which, when pronounced together
sounded like consonants with a "✓" above them. Such letters
are č-spelled as cz, or tsch (Kubíček-Kovitschek, Zajíčko-
vic-Zagieczkowitc, Slavíček-Slawitschek, Spička-Spitschka),
and ř, spelled as rz (Příkopa-Przikopa, Kopriva-Koprziwa).
In the case of vowels, e would have been spelled as ie
(Věrný-Wierny).

Such phonetic spellings may have been given to Czech names
in America to replace diacritical marks not used in the
English alphabet. Some Czech immigrants did not want to
change their names; in fact, they were sensitive about
their correct pronunciation of their family surnames so
they adjusted spellings to make it possible for their
American neighbors to pronounce their names correctly.
Kopřiva might have been spelled Koprziva or Černý, Czerný.
This does not change the names too much; however, when
doing research in Czechoslovakian records, one has to keep
in mind that either spelling may appear.

From the foregoing it is evident that there are as many
surnames in the Bohemian lands as there are nouns, adjectives,
adverbs and their derivatives. As recently as one hundred
years ago it was possible to assume that a certain surname
was confined to a given locality or area. This changed,
of course, as the people became more mobile. For a century
now, the people have moved around; many went to school,
found jobs, or married and settled in new areas, which destroyed any regional identification of the surname. It is
difficult to assume that one Czech surname is more prevalent
or frequent than others.

The Czech language, unlike English, is sensitive to gender.
The Czech surname for a male may end in a consonant, indicating that it is a noun, or in "ý" which is the masculine
ending of an adjective. To indicate the feminine gender, an
"ova" will appear at the end of the noun and "a" at the
end of the adjective.

> Kováč-Kováčova,   Černý-Černá
> Sedlák-Sedláková   Malý-Malá

In instances where the male version of the surname ends with
a consonant preceded by an "e", this "e" in the female case
is dropped:

> Komárek-Komárkoyá
> Roubíček-Roubíčková

There are some nouns that later became surnames, which end
in "e," or "ů." These do not change in the female versions:

> Krejčí-Krejčí
> Sousední-Sousední
> Janů-Janů
> Jírků-Jírků

Up to about 1850 one might find a woman listed in the matriky with the surname of her father or husband in a German
female version, that is, with the suffix in added to the
male surname:

> Sedlák-Sedlákin
> Černý-Černýin

In official documents, a married woman is usually listed
by her given name and her husband's family name, followed
by her maiden name, preceded by "rozená"--born (abbreviated
roz.):

> Věra Megová, roz. Roubíčková

In documents or matriky the title Pan (Mister) is not used
unless the individual was a member of the nobility, in which
case he would be referred to as Urozený pán (well-born
mister). Paní (Mrs.) is seldom used and only if reference

is made to the wife of a nobleman. The equivalent of the word "miss" is slečna, which came into usage later in the nineteenth century. Before this, an unmarried woman was referred to as panna (virgin); if the minister or his clerk had any doubts as to the right of the woman to this title, he would cruelly state so in the matriky.

There are few instances of double or hyphenated surnames, and these appear only among the names of prominent people who were given a special, official approval for this change. In modern times changing the surname is difficult; one has to have a court decision for this and prove very valid reasons for the change.

There are also very few instances of more than one given name for an individual in one family; the only exception to this is the name Maří (form of Marie) Magdalena, or Jan Blahoslav or Jan Nepomucký. These exceptions are linked to the customary reverence for saints in the Catholic church. There were more than one Maří or Jan canonized in the church; this was usually designated by a double name. The second name has seldom been used by the individual. It is important for genealogical research, as a family could have had two children by the name, Maří or Jan with both living to maturity. Unless the second name is mentioned in the matriky when the person married, it is difficult to discern which of the Maříis or Jans married your direct ancestor or ancestress.

Traditionally, names of the saints of the Roman Catholic Church were chosen as křestní (christening) names. However, after World War I in Bohemia and, to a lesser degree in Moravia, there was a movement away from Rome, as evidenced by the founding of the Czechoslovakian church in 1920, which did not recognize the pope as its head. Participants in this movement chose names for their children from among the old Slavonic given names and avoided using traditional saints' names. Typically, the old Slavonic names include the suffixes: -slav (glory), -mír (peace), -mil (love), and -bor (forest) as in:

Masculine	Feminine
Bohuslav	Bohuslava
Jaroslav	Jaroslava
Bohumír	Bohumíra
Jaromír	Jaromíra
Bohumil	Bohumila
Vlastimil	Vlastimila
Dalibor	Dalibora
Ctibor	Ctibora

As indicated earlier, most Czech masculine given names, of all origins, end in a consonant, unless the name is a diminutive; and Czech feminine given names usually end in -a, or occasionally, in a consonant (for example, Dagmar).

Diminutives are not used officially, and therefore will not be found in the matriky or old documents.

The given names in Czechoslovakian records appear in three versions, Czech (or Slovak), Latin, or German. I have tried to locate a comparative list of these given names in the three languages with the intention of adding their English equivalents. Apparently no such list exists. Thus the following is a first attempt at compiling this comparative list. Any additions or corrections will be gratefully received.

For the compilation of Czech given names, I have used annual calendars. As a rule they contain the name of a saint for each day of the year, unless the day is designated as a national or Catholic Church holiday. I also used the 1976 calendar České Nebe, církevní rodinný kalendář,[1] and the 1976 calendar published in Československý svět (Czechoslovakian World)[2]. With few exceptions they all agree. To those I added the names listed in CZECH PERSONAL NAMES, compiled by the Central Intelligence Agency, Washington, D.C., 1964. Also included are names I have noted in my many years of experience in genealogical research, as well as those taken from historical writings. Consequently there are many more given names in this listing in Czech than in Slovak. To obtain a listing of the given names in the Slovak version, I used SLOVAK PERSONAL NAMES as compiled by the Central Intelligence Agency.

I had considerable difficulty in obtaining the Latin versions of both Czech and Slovak given names, as none have been compiled. However, it appears that the priests or clerks of the Catholic parishes in the past were not much more informed than I on the translation of difficult Czech and Slovak given names into Latin; so in many instances they simply added the suffix -us or -ius to a male given name, which to them looked Latin enough. Gardner and Smith's GENEALOGICAL RESEARCH IN ENGLAND AND WALES, vol. 3, was of great help in finding the English equivalents of Czech given names (see bibliography following this chapter). In the listing I leave out the Latinized versions of the names, giving them only in instances where they differ significantly. The English language has more versions for modern Czech and Slovak given names than for the old Slavonic names. Typical suffixes of such names have been given earlier in this chapter. One can assume that in the majority of instances the male name had a female version created simply by adding -a.

---

1. Czech Heaven, church family calendar. Published by Česká Katolická Misie in Los Angeles, California.
2. Publication of the Czechoslovakian Foreign Institute, Prague I, Malá Strana, Karmelitská 25, 118-31.

Names

To the Americans whose ancestors came from Czechoslovakia,
I suggest that they look at the English versions first,
then at the Czech or Slovak equivalent, thus arriving at
the possible original given name of their ancestor. For
example, Larry, which is an abbreviation of Lawrence,
might have been Vavřinec.

For compiling the German versions of the Czech and Slovak
given names, I used Dr. Ernst Wasserzieher's HANS UND
GRETE; however, I listed only those that I was sure of.
No doubt there are others.

I hope that this list, incomplete as it may be, will prove
helpful to those in quest of their Czechoslovakian ancestors.

MALE

Czech	Slovak	Latin	German	English
Abel	Abel		Abel	Abel
Abraham			Abraham	Abraham
Absɔlom			Absalom	Absalom
Adam	Adam		Adam	Adam
Adolf	Adolf		Adolf	Adolph
Alán				Allan
Albert	Albert		Albert	Albert
				Elbert
Albín	Albín		Albin	Albin
Albrecht				Albrecht
Aleksandr	Alexander		Alexander	Alexander
Ales	Ales			
Alex				
Alexej				
Alfons	Alfonz		Alfons	Alphonse
Alfréd	Alfréd	Alberedus	Alfred	Alfred
		Aluredus		
Alois	Alojz	Aloysius	Alois	
Amát				
Ambróž	Ambróz			Ambrose
Amos	Amos		Amos	Amos
Anatol				Anatole
Andrej	Andrej		Andreas	Andrew
Antonín	Anton		Anton	Anthony
Arcibald				Archibald
Arnold				
Arnošt	Arnošt		Ernst	Ernest
Aron	Aron		Aaron	Aaron
	Arpád			
Artúr	Artúr	Arcturius	Arthur	Arthur
Atanás	Athanás			Athanasius
August	August		August	Austin
Augustín	Augustín			Agustus
	Aurel			

86

Czech	Slovak	Latin	German	English

FEMALE

Czech	Slovak	Latin	German	English
Ada	Ada		Ada	
Adéla				Adelle
Agáta	Agáta		Agatha	Agatha
Albína	Albína			
Aleksandra			Alexandra	Alexandra
Alena				
Alice	Alica	Aelizia	Alice	Alice
		Alesia		
Aloisie				
Alžběta	Alžbeta		Elisabetha	Elisabeth
			(many other versions)	
Amálie	Amália		Amalie	Amelia
Anabela		Anabilia		Annabel
Anastázie	Anastázia		Anastasia	Anastasia
Anděla	Andela			
Andrea			Andrea	Andrea
Aneta (Anita)	Anita			
Anežka	Anežka			
Anna	Anna		Anna	Ann
Antonie	Antonia		Antonie	
Apoléna or	Apolónia		Apollonie	Apollonia
Apolónie				
Arabela			Arabella	Arabella
Arleta				
Arnoštka				Ernestine
Augusta	Augusta			Augusta

MALE

Czech	Slovak	Latin	German	English
Baltazar			Balthasar	Balthasar
Barnabáš	Barnabáš		Barnabas	Barnaby
Bartoloměj	Bartolomej	Bartholomaus		Bartholomew
Bedřich	Bedrich		Friedrich	Frederick
Benedikt	Beňadik		Benedict	Benedict
Beno			Benno	
Bernard	Bernard		Bernhard	Bernard
Bivoj				
Blahomil				
Blahomír	Blahomír			
Blahorád				
Blahoslav	Blahoslav			
Blahut				
Blažej		Blasius	Blase	Blaise
Bohdan	Bohdan			
Bohumil	Bohumil	Amadeus	Gottlieb	Theophil
			Theophil	
Bohumír	Bohumír	Godefridus	Gottfried	Godfrey
Bohurad	Bohurad			
Bohuš				
Bohuslav	Bohuslav		Botthold	

Names

Czech	Slovak	Latin	German	English
Boleslav			Boleslaw	
Bonifác		Bonifactius		
Boreš				
Boris			Boris	Boris
	Borislav			
Bořivoj	Borivoj			
Božej				
Bozetěch				
Břetislav				
Bronislav	Branislav			
Bruno	Bruno			Bruno

FEMALE

Czech	Slovak	Latin	German	English
Barbora	Barbora		Barbara	Barbara
Bedřiška				Fredericka
Běla				
Berta			Berta	Bertha
Blahomila				
Blahoslava	Blahoslava			
Blanka	Blanka			Blanche
Blažena	Blazena			
Bohdana	Bohdana			
Bohumila				
Bohunka				
Boleslava				
Božena		Beatricia, Beatrix	Beatrice	Beatrice
Břetislava				
Brigita	Brigita		Brigitte	Brigitta
Bronislava	Branislava		Bronislawa	Bernice

MALE

Czech	Slovak	Latin	German	English
Cecil	Cecil	Caecilius Seisillas	Cecil	Cecil
Celestýn	Celestin			
Čeněk				
Česlav				
	Céres			Ceres
Čestmír	Cestmir			
Chrudoš				
	Ctiboh			
Ctibor	Ctibor			
Ctirád				
Ctislav				
Cyprián	Cyprián	Zyprianus		
Cyril	Cyril			Cyril
	Cyrus			

Czech	Slovak	Latin	German	English

FEMALE

Cecilie	Cecilia	Caecilia	Cecilia	Cecily
Celestína	Celestina	Coelestina	Celestina	Celestina
Česta				
Čestmíra				

MALE

Dalibor	Dalibor			
Dalimil				
Dalimír				
Damaš				
	Damián	Dominitius	Damian	
Daniel	Daniel		Daniel	Daniel
David	David		David	David
	Demeter			
Denis		Dionysius		Dennis
Depold				
	Dezider		Desider	
	Dionýz			Dennis
Diviš	Diviš			
Dobromil	Dobromil			
Dobroslav	Dobroslav			
Dominik	Dominik		Dominic	Dominic
	Donát			
	Dorotej			
	Drabotin			
Drahomír	Drahomír			
Drahoslav	Drahoslav			
Duchoslav				
Dušan	Dušan			

FEMALE

Dagmar	Dagmara		Dagmar	
Dalimila	Dalmila			
Dana	Dana			
	Darina			
Daniela	Daniela		Daniela	Daniela
Daša				
Denisa				
Dita	Ditta			
Dobromila	Dobromila			
Dobroslava	Dobroslava			
	Dobrotka			
	Dobruša			
Dora				
Dorota	Dorota	Dorothea	Dorothea	Dorothy
Doubravka				

Names

Czech	Slovak	Latin	German	English
Drahomíra	Drahomira			
Drahoslava	Drahoslava			
	Dubravka			
Duchoslava				
Dušana				

MALE

Czech	Slovak	Latin	German	English
Edgar	Edgar			Edgar
Edmund	Edmund			Edmund
Eduard,Edvard	Eduard			Edward
	Egid	Aegidius		
	Egon			
Eliáš	Eliáš			Elias
	Elo			
Emanuel	Emanuel	Immanuel		
Emerich			Emmerich	
Emil	Emil	Aemilius	Emil	Emil
	Emilián			
	Enoch			
Erazím				
	Erhard			
Erik	Erik		Erich	Eric
Ernest	Ernest		Ernst	Ernest
Ervín	Ervín			Irwin
Eusebius				
Eustas	Eustas			
Evžen,Eugen	Eugen		Eugen	Eugene

FEMALE

Czech	Slovak	Latin	German	English
Edita	Edita		Edith	Edith
Ela	Ella		Ella	Ella
Eleanora	Eleonora		Eleanor	Eleanor
Elena	Elena			Ellen
Eliška	Eliška			
Ema	Ema		Emma	
	Erika			
Emilie	Emilia	Emelina	Emilie	Emily
Ester	Ester		Esther	Esther
	Etela			
Eulalie	Eulalia		Eulalia	Eulalia
Evženie	Eugenia		Eugenie	Eugenia

MALE

Czech	Slovak	Latin	German	English
Fabián	Fabian		Fabian	Fabian
	Faustin		Faustin	Faustus
	Fedor			
Felix	Felix			Felix

Czech	Slovak	Latin	German	English
Ferdinand	Ferdinand		Ferdinand	Ferdinand
Fidel			Fidel	
Filip	Filip		Philip	Philip
Flavián				
Florián	Florian		Florian	Florian
Fortunát				
František	František	Franziskus	Franz	Frank, Francis

FEMALE

Flora				Flora
Františka	Františka			Frances

MALE

Gabriel	Gabriel		Gabriel	Gabriel
Gašpar	Gašpar		Kaspar	Casper
	Gejza			
	Gerard			
	Gerazim			
	Gerhard			
	Gorazd			
	Gregor			Gregory
Gustav	Gustav			Augustus

FEMALE

Gabriela	Gabriela		Gabriele	Gabriela
Galena	Galina			
Gertuda	Gertruda		Gertrud	Gertrude
	Genovefa		Genoveva	Genevieve
Gizela	Gizela		Gisella	Giselle
Gustina				

MALE

	Hadrian		Adrian	Adrian or Hadrian
Hanuš				
Haštal				
Havel				Gallus
	Helmut			
Herbert	Herbert		Herbert	Herbert
Herman	Herman		Hermann	Herman
	Horislav			
	Horus			Horace
Horymír				
Hostimil	Hostimil			
Hostivít	Hostivít			

Names

Czech	Slovak	Latin	German	English
Hubert	Hubert		Hubert	Hubert
Hugo	Hugo		Hugo	Hugh
Hvězdoslav	Hvezdoň			
	Hyginus			
Hypolit				

FEMALE

Czech	Slovak	Latin	German	English
Halka				
Hana	Hana	Johanne		Hanna
	Hajnal			
Háta				
Hedvika	Hedviga		Hedwig	Hedwiga
Helena	Helena		Helene	Helen
Hermína	Hermína		Hermine	
Hilda			Hilde	Hilda
	Horislava			
Hvězdoslava				

MALE

Czech	Slovak	Latin	German	English
Ignác	Ignác	Ignatius	Ignaz	
	Igor			
Ilja	Ilja			
	Imrich		Imre	Emerich
Inocenc	Innocent			
Ivan	Ivan	Johannes	Johannes	John
Ivo	Ivo			
	Izakiáš			Isaiah
Izák	Izák			Isaac
	Izidor			Isidore

FEMALE

Czech	Slovak	Latin	German	English
Ida	Ida		Ida	Ida
	Ifigénia			
Ilona				
	Ilza		Ilse	Elsa
Iréna	Iréna		Irene	Irene
Irma	Irma			Irma
Isabella	Izabela		Elisabeth	Isabella
Iva	Ivica			
Ivana				
Iveta				Yvette

MALE

Czech	Slovak	Latin	German	English
Jachým, Joachim	Joachim		Joachim	Joachim

Czech	Slovak	Latin	German	English
Jakub	Jakub		Jacob	James
				Jacob
Jan	Jan	Johannes	Johannes	John
			Hans	
Januar				
Januš				
Jarolím	Jarolím			
Jaromil,				
Jarmil				
Jaromír				
Jaroslav	Jaroslav			
Jeroným	Jeremiaš	Hieremias	Jeremias	Jeremiah
Jiljí				
Jindřich		Henrycus	Heinrich	Henry
Jiří	Juraj	Georgius	Georg	George
Jób	Jób		Job	Job
Jonatán	Jonatán			Jonathan
	Jordán			
Josef	Jozef		Joseph	Joseph
	Juda			
Julián	Julián			Julian
Julius	Julius		Julius	Julius
Jura				
Justýn				Justin

FEMALE

Czech	Slovak	Latin	German	English
	Jadviga		Hedwig	Hedvica
Jana	Jana	Johanna	Johanna	Jane
Jarmila				
Jaroslava	Jaroslava			
Jaruška				
Jasněna				
Jenovéfa	Jela,			Genevieve
	Jelena,			
	Genoveva			
Jindřiška				
Jiřina				Georgina
Jiška				
Jitka,	Judita		Judith	Judith
Judita				
Johana,				
Jana			Jolanthe	
Jolana			Josepha	Josephine
Josefa,	Jozefina			
Josefina				
Juliána				
Julie	Julia		Julie	Julie
	Justina		Justine	Justine

93

Names

Czech	Slovak	Latin	German	English
MALE				
Kajetán	Kajetán	Cajetan		
Kalista	Kalixt			
Kamil	Kamil			
Karel	Karol	Carl, Carolus	Karl	Charles
Kašpar	Gašpar			Casper
Kazimír	Kazimír	Casimir		
Klement	Klement			Clement
	Kleofáš			
	Koloman			
Klimeš				
Kochan				
Konrád	Konrád		Conrad	Conrad
Konstantýn	Konstantín			Constantine
Kosma,				
Kosmas				
	Kornel			Cornell
Krasoslav	Krasoslav			
Křesimír				
Křesomysl				
	Krišpín			Crispin
Kristán,	Kristián		Christian	Christian
Kristián,				
Kristýn				
Kryštof	Krištof			Christopher
Kurt				Curtis
	Květoslav			
Kvido				
	Kvirín			
FEMALE				
Kamila	Kamila			Camille
Karla,	Karla		Carla	Caroline
Karolína	Karolína			
Kateřina	Katarína		Katharine	Catherine
Klára,	Klára			Clara,
Klarisa				Clarissa
Klementína				Clementine
Klotylda			Klothilde	Clotilde
Kornelia	Kornelia			Cornelia
Krasava	Kráska			
Krasoslava	Krasoslava			
Kristýna	Kristína			Christine
Kunhuta				
Květa,	Květoslava			Flora
Květoslava,				
Kvetuše				

Czech	Slovak	Latin	German	English
MALE				
Ladislav, Vladislav	Ladislav		Ladislaus	Leslie
Lambert	Lambert		Lambert	Lambert
	Laurinec, Vavřinec		Laurens	Lawrence
Lazar	Lazar			
Leo, Leoš	Leo			Leon
Leonard	Leonard	Lionhardus	Leonhard	Leonard
Leopold	Leopold			Leopold
Lev	Lev			Lionel
	Levoslav			
Lešek				
Lexa				
Libor, Lubor	Lubor			
Linhart, Leonhard			Lienhard	Leonard
Lubomír				
Luboš	Luboš			
	Luboslav			
Lucian				
Luděk				
Ludevít, Ludvík	Ludovít, Ludvík		Ludwig	Ludwig
Lukáš		Lucas		Luke
Lumír				
FEMALE				
Lada	Lada			
Ladislava	Ladislava			Leslie
Laura	Laura		Laura	Laura
Lea			Lea	Leah
Lena, Lenka	Lenka		Lene	Lena
Leona			Leonie	
Leontyna	Leontina			
	Leopoldína		Leopolda	
Libena				
Libuše	Libuša		Libussa	
	Lubica			
Lidmila				
Linda				Linda
Ljuba			Lioba	
Lubomíra				
Lucie	Lucia		Lucia	Lucy
Ludmila	Ludmila		Ludmilla	
Lujza	Lujza		Louise	Louise
	Lukrécia			Lucretia
Lydia	Lydia		Lydia	Lydia

Names

Czech	Slovak	Latin	German	English

MALE

Czech	Slovak	Latin	German	English
Malachius, Malachiáš	Malachiáš			Malachias
	Manfréd		Manfred	Manfred
Mansvet				
	Manuel			
Marcel	Marcel		Marcel	Marcel
	Marcián			
Marek	Marek	Marcus	Mark	Mark
Martin	Martin		Martin	Martin
Matěj	Matěj	Mattheus	Matthias	Matthew
Matouš	Matuš			Matthias
Matyáš				
Maxim, Mazimilián	Maxin		Maximilian	Maximilian
Mečislav	Maximilián			
Medard			Medard	
Melichar	Melichar		Melchior	Melchior
Metoděj	Metod			Methodus
Michal	Michal		Michael	Michael
Mikuláš	Mikuláš	Nicolaus		Nicholas
Milan	Milan			
Milodar				
Miloš	Miloš			
Miloslav	Miloslav			
Miroslav	Miro			
	Milutín			
Milovan				
	Mladen			
Mojmír, Mojžíš	Mojžíš	Moyses	Moses	Moses
Móric	Móric	Mauritius	Moritz	Maurice
Mstislav				

FEMALE

Czech	Slovak	Latin	German	English
Magdalena	Magdalena		Magdalene	Magdalene
Malvina	Malvina		Lawine	Malvina
Marcela	Marcela		Marcella	Marcella
Mariana	Mariana			Marianne
Marie	Mária		Maria	Mary
Marína	Marína		Marina, Maren	Marina
Markéta	Margita		Margareta	Margaret
Marta	Marta		Martha	Martha
Matylda	Matilda		Mathilde	Matilda
Melanie	Melanie		Melanie	Melanie
Michaela	Michaela		Michaela	
Milada	Milada			
Milena	Milena			
Miloslava, Miluše	Miloslava			

Czech	Slovak	Latin	German	English
Miroslava				
	Milica			
Mlada				
Monika	Monika		Monika	Monica

MALE

Narcis				Narciss
Neklan				
Nepomuk				
	Nestor			
Nezamysl				
	Nikifor			
Nikodém	Nikodém			Nicodemus
Nikol				Nicola
Norbert	Norbert		Norbert	Norbert

FEMALE

Naďa	Naďa			
Naděžda	Naděžda			
Narcisa				
Natalje,	Natalje,			
Nataša	Nataša			
Nikola				
Nina				Nina
Nora				Nora
Norberta				

MALE

Oktávián				
Oldřich	Oldrich			
Oleg	Olek			
Ondřej	Ondřej		Andreas	Andrew
	Orest			
Oskar	Oskar		Oskar	Oscar
Osvald			Oswald	Oswald
Otakar			Ottokar	
Otmar	Otmar		Otmar	
Oto	Oto		Otto	Otto

FEMALE

Oldřiška				
Olga			Olga	Olga
Olivia			Olivia	Olive
Otilie	Otilia			Otilla

Names

Czech	Slovak	Latin	German	English
MALE				
Pankrác	Pankrác		Pankraz	
	Panteleon		Pantaleon	
Patrík	Patrík			Patrick
Pavel	Pavol		Paul	Paul
Petr	Peter		Peter	Peter
Polykarp	Polykarp		Polykarp	
	Porfýr			
Pravolub	Pravolub			
Pravoslav	Pravoslav			
Předislav				
Přemek				
Přemysl				
Příbek				
Přibyslav				
Prokop	Prokop		Prokop	Procopius
FEMALE				
Patricie				Patricia
Pavla,	Pavla,		Pauline	Pauline
Pavlína	Paulína			
	Perla			Pearl
Petra				
Petronela			Petronella	Petronella
Petruška,				
Petriška				
	Pira			
Pravoslava	Pravoslava			
Přibyslava				
	Prudencia		Prudencia	Prudence
MALE				
Rádek,				
Rádko				
Radim				
Radomil,	Radomil			
Radim				
Radomír	Radomír			
Radoslav	Radoslav			
Radovan				
Rafael	Rafael		Raphael	Raphael
Rajmund	Rajmund		Reimund	Raymond
Rastislav	Rastislav			
Ratibor	Ratibor			
	Ratmír			
Raul				Ralph
Řehoř	Gregor			Gregory
Remeš				

98

Czech	Slovak	Latin	German	English
René				
Richard	Richard		Richard	Richard
Robert	Robert		Robert	Robert
Roman	Roman		Roman	Roman
Rostislav				
Rudolf	Rudolf		Rudolf	Rudolph
Rufus			Rufus	Rufus
Rupert	Rupert		Rupert	

FEMALE

Rachel	Rachel		Rachel	Rachel
Radislava				
Radka				
Radmila,				
Radomila				
Radoslava	Radoslava			
Rafaela			Raphaela	Raphaela
Regina	Regína		Regine	Regina
Renáta	Renáta		Renate	Renata
Roberta			Roberta	Roberta
Rostislava				
Rozálie	Rozália			Rosalie
Rút	Rút		Ruth	Ruth
Ruzena	Ruzena		Rosa	Rose

MALE

Sabín	Sabín			Sabin
Salomon	Salomon		Salomon	Solomon
	Samson,		Samson	Sampson
	Sampson			
Samuel	Samuel		Samuel	Samuel
Saturnín				
Šebek				
Sergej		Sergius		
Servác	Servác			
Severín	Severín		Severin	Severin
	Sigfríd		Siegfried	
Silvestr,	Silvester,		Silvester	Sylvester
Sylvestr	Sylvester			
Šimon	Šimeon		Simon	Simon
Slavata				
Slavibor				
Slavoj				
Slavomír	Slavomír			
Smil				
Soběslav				
Spythihněv				
Stanislav	Stanislav			Stanley
Stašek				

Names

Czech	Slovak	Latin	German	English
Střezimír				
Svatoboj				
Svatopluk				
Svatoslav				
	Svetozár			

FEMALE

Czech	Slovak	Latin	German	English
Sabína	Sabína		Sabine	Sabina
	Sába			
Sana				
Sára	Sára		Sara	Sarah
Šárka				
	Sarolta			Charlotte
Sáva	Sáva			
Silvia	Silvia		Silvia	Silvia
Šimona			Simone	Simone
Slavěna	Slávia			
Slavomíra	Slavomíra			
Soběslava				
	Sofie		Sophia	Sophie
Soňa			Sonja	Sonja
Stanislava				
Stela			Stella	Stella
Štěpánka	Stefánia		Stephanie	Stephanie
Svata,				
Svatoslava				
Světla				

MALE

Czech	Slovak	Latin	German	English
Tadeáš			Thadeus	Thaddeus
Teodor	Teodor		Theodor	Theodore
	Teofil		Theophil	Theophil
Těšivoj				
	Tibor			
	Tichomír			
Timotěj	Timotěj			Timothy
	Titus		Titus	Titus
Tomáš	Tomáš		Thomas	Thomas

FEMALE

Czech	Slovak	Latin	German	English
Tamara			Tamara	
Taťána	Taťána		Tatiana	Tatiana
Tekla	Tekla		Thekla	Thekla
Terezie	Terezia		Theresia	Teresa

Czech	Slovak	Latin	German	English
MALE				
Urban	Urban		Urban	Urban
FEMALE				
Uršula	Uršula		Ursule	Ursula
MALE				
Václav	Václav		Wenceslaus	Wenceslaus
Valburg				
Valdemar			Waldemar	Waldemar
Valentýn	Valent		Valentin	Valentine
Valerián				
Vasil	Vazil			Basil
Valter,	Valter	Galterus	Walter	Walter
Valtr				
Vavřinec	Vavrinec			Lawrence
Velen				
Veleslav	Veleslav			
Vendelín	Vendelín		Wendelin	Wendel
Věroslav	Vieroslav			
Viktor	Viktor		Viktor	Victor
Viktorín	Viktorín			
Vilém	Viliam	Guillelmus	Wilhelm	William
Vilibald				
Vincenc	Vincent		Vincent	Vincent
Virgil			Virgil	Virgil
Vít	Vít	Wildo	Vit	Guy
Vítězslav	Vítázoslav			
Vladan,				
Vladimír	Vladimír			
Vladislav,	Vladislav			
Ladislav				
Vladivoj,				
Vládko				
Vlastimil	Vlastimil			
Vlastislav	Vlastislav			
Vnislav				
Vojslav				
Vojtěch	Vojtěch		Adalbert	Adalbert
Volnomil				
Vratislav	Vratislav			
	Všemil			
Vuk				
FEMALE				
Václava,				
Vendulka				

Names

Czech	Slovak	Latin	German	English
Valburga				
Valérie	Valéria		Valerie	Valery
Valentína	Valentína		Valentine	Valentine
Vanda				
Vendunka				
Věnceslava				
Věra	Viera		Vera	Vera
Veronika	Verona		Verena	Veronica
Věroslava	Vieroslava			
Viktorie	Viktoria		Viktoria	Victoria
Vilemína,	Vilma			Wilma
Vilma				
Viola	Viola		Viola	Viola
Vítězslava	Vítězslava			
Vlasta	Vlasta			
Vlastimila	Vlastimila			
Vlastislava	Vlastislava			
Voršila,			Ursule	Ursula
Uršula				
Vratislava	Vratislava			

MALE

Czech	Slovak	Latin	German	English
Xaver,	Xaver		Xaver	Xavier
Ksaver				
Xenofón,	Xenofón			
Ksenofón				
Xerxes,	Xerxes			
Kserkses				

FEMALE

Czech	Slovak	Latin	German	English
Xantipa,	Xantipa			
Ksantipa				
Xénia,	Xénia			
Ksénia				

MALE

Czech	Slovak	Latin	German	English
Záboj				
Zachariáš	Zachariáš		Zacharias	Zacharias
Závis				
Zbihněv				
Zbislav				
Zbyněk	Zbyněk			
Zdeněk	Zdeno		Sidonius	Sideon
Zdirad				
Želimir				
Želislav	Želislav			
Zikmund	Zigmund			
Žitomír	Žitomír			

Czech	Slovak	Latin	German	English
Zlatko	Zlatan			
	Zvonimír			

FEMALE

Czech	Slovak	Latin	German	English
Zaja				
Zdenka	Zdenka		Sidonie	Sidonia
Zdislava				
Zelimíra	Zelmíra			
Zina				
Zita	Zita		Zita	
Ziva				
Zlata,	Zlátka			
Zlátka				
Žofie	Žofia		Sophie	Sophie
Zora	Zora			
Zuzana	Zuzana		Susanna	Susan

BIBLIOGRAPHY

Beneš, Josef. O ČESKÝCH PŘÍJMENÍCH. Prague: n.p., 1962.
GL 943.7 B4s. In Czech.

Analytical work, listing a number of Czech surnames
and giving their origin.

Bennett, Archibald F. A GUIDE FOR GENEALOGICAL RESEARCH.
Salt Lake City: Deseret News Press, 1951. GL 929.1 B439g

An excellent account of various genealogical sources.
Its great value lies in numerous supplements, such
as genealogical expressions in several languages
(Slavic languages excluded), Latin counting, and
Latin given names with their English equivalents.

Curín, František. "Z Dějin Českých Osobních Jmén. Křestní
Jména Oblíbená v 15. a 16. Století". NAŠE REC no. 32
(1948): 76-83.

Flajšhans, Václav. "Naše Nejstarší Jména Osobní." NAŠE
REC nos. 10-12, (1926): 257-66, 193-97, 169-74.

Gardner, David and Smith, Frank. GENEALOGICAL RESEARCH IN
ENGLAND AND WALES. Vol. 3. Salt Lake City: Bookcraft, 1964.
GL 929.142 G172g.

Contains an appendix listing Latin given names with
their English equivalents.

Hráše, J.K. "PRAJMÉNA ČESKÝCH ŽEN. No. 4. Prague: Ženské
Listy, 1883.

Czech women's ancient names. Doubtful that it is still available.

Horecký, J. GRECKÉ A LATINSKÉ VLASTNÉ MÉNA V SLOVENČTINE. S.R. vol. 12. N.p., 1946. In Slovak.

Greek and Latin given names in Slovakian.

Hulakovský, J.M. O PŮVODU A PROMĚNÁCH JMÉN RODNÍCH. N.p. 1860. In Czech.

Origin and changes of family names.

_____, PŘÍJMENÍ ČESKÁ VZNIKLÁ ZE JMÉN KŘESTNÍCH. Program Gymnasia ve Spálené ulici v Praze, 1888-89. In Czech.

Collective work of the students at the Gymnasium School in Spálená ulice, Prague. Czech surnames that originated from given names.

"O Českých Příjmeních." STUDIE A PRAMENY. Vol. 14. In Czech.

Concerning Czech surnames.

Palacký, František. "Popis Staročeských Osobních a Křestních Jmén." CCm (1932): 59-60. In Czech.

Discussion of ancient Czech given names.

Prášek, V. O JMÉNECH RODINNÝCH. Prague: Komenský, 1874. In Czech.

Concerning surnames.

Schwarz, E. SUDETENDEUTSCHE FAMILIENNAMEN AUS VORHUSITIS-CHER ZEIT. Koeln-Graz, 1957. In German.

Surnames of the Sudeten area before the Hussite wars.

"Starobylá Jména Našich Předků." ČESKÁ ŠKOLA 5 (1883). In Czech.

Ancient names of our forefathers.

Starodávné Osobné Mená Slovenské." SLOVENSKÝ JAZYK (1940). In Slovakian.

Ancient Slovakian given names.

Svoboda, Jan. STAROČESKÁ OSOBNÍ JMÉNA A NAŠE PŘÍJMENÍ. Prague: N.p., 1964. GL 929.4 Sv51j or microfilm 496,595 (second item). In Czech.

Ancient Czech given names and surnames.

Teplý, František. "O Původu a Změnách Příjmení." CASOPIS
RODOPISNÉ SPOLEČNOSTI V PRAZE 16:5. In Czech.

   Article about the origin and changes of Czech surnames.

_____. "Různosti Českých Příjmení." ČASOPIS
RODOPISNÉ SPOLEČNOSTI V PRAZE. 16: 20.

   Variations of Czech surnames.

Trávníček, F. "Vlastní Substantiva." SBORNÍK PRACÍ
FILOSOFICKÉ FAKULTY BRNĚNSKÉ UNIVERSITY, JAZYKOVĚDNE A
no. 5-9, (1958). In Czech.

   Czech surnames as nouns.

Trávníček, F., and Svoboda, J. "Dobrovskeho Studium
Vlastních Jmén." SBORNÍK JOSEF DOBROVSKY, 1753 (1953).
In Czech.

   Josef Dobrovský was a leading filolog of the late
   eighteenth century. This booklet deals with his
   study of Czech given names.

Wasserzieher, Ernst. HANS UND GRETE. Bonn, Germany: GL
929.43 W283h. In German.

   Origin of German given names and their variations.

Chapter 8
THE CALENDAR

The calendar is a system for dividing and recording time.
There are two great natural divisions of time--the day and
the year, both based on the relative positions of the earth
and the sun. The month is based on the changing appearance
of the moon in the sky. The week is a man-made division
of time, based on the division of the lunar cycle, however,
the number of days in a week was first mentioned in the
book of Genesis in the Bible.

Prompted by astrologists and their findings, there were
several attempts in ancient times to establish a calendar.
The various nations, however, each calculated the division
of time according to their own figures, which made an in-
telligent and reliable recording on an international basis
impossible. On the advice of his astrologers, the Roman
Emperor Julius Caesar ordered the preparation of a system-
atic calendar in 46 B.C. Although there were many defi-
ciencies and errors, this Julian calendar was used for many
centuries by all Christian nations.

In 1582, Pope Gregory XIII reformed the errors of the Julian
calendar by introducing a new calendar, called the Gregorian Calendar, which is still in use. The Gregorian calendar was adopted almost immediately by all the Catholic
nations of Europe; but the Protestant nations were slow to
accept it. This led to confusion regarding the exact date
of certain important events because the correction of the
Julian calendar created a discrepancy of ten days between
the two systems. For example, the date of 5 October 1582
on the Julian calendar became 15 October 1582 on the Gregorian calendar.

The Catholic part of Switzerland accepted the Gregorian
calendar in 1584, while the Protestant part only in 1700;
England in 1752 (this includes America, which at that time
was a British possession); and Sweden in 1753. There were
some nations which did not accept the Gregorian calendar
until the twentieth century: Russia, Albania, Bulgaria,
Turkey, and Rumania.

There were some problems and difficulties with the calendar
in the Czech lands, also. Following the mandate of Emperor

Rudolph II, Bohemia adopted the Gregorian calendar. The Moravians, on the other hand, claimed that this mandate was issued before its official approval by the Congress and therefore waited for nine months before they accepted the new calendar. During this nine-month period, the dates of certain national or regional events will differ from Bohemia to Moravia. Following are the dates of the adoption of the new calendar in various parts of present-day Czechoslovakia:

> Bohemia: accepted 6 January 1584. The date of the following day was 17 January 1584.

> Moravia: accepted 4 October 1584. The date of the following day was 14 October 1584.

> Silesia: accepted 12 January 1584. The date of the following day was 23 January 1584.

> Slovakia: accepted 21 October 1587. The date of the following day was 1 November 1587.

For the American searching for his Czechoslovakian ancestry, these dates are very important in the study of ancient records and documents. Many documents simply do not mention the change of calendar and dates. If the scribe in the records did mention the change in the calendar, he would use these Latin expressions: More novo (new reckoning) and more vetere (old reckoning).

Of great importance for genealogical research in Czechoslovakia is the knowledge of the Catholic feasts commemorating certain events or deeds of the saints. With the exception of Easter and the feasts calculated around it, the days of feasts do not change from year to year, so they are marked on every printed calendar. Many documents and matriky list the names of these holidays in preference to an actual date. Therefore, unless you can translate the name of such a holiday into an actual calendar date, all you can glean from such an entry is the year.

Below are listed some such holidays as they might be entered in the matriky, in Latin, with their Czech equivalents, If in existence, and also the day of the year when they occur:

Latin	Czech	Date
Adventio		Sunday nearest 30 November
Annunciato		25 March
Ascention Domini	Nanebevzetí Páně	Thursday, forty days after Easter Sunday
Assumption	Nanebevzetí Panny Marie	15 August

Latin	Czech	Date
Cantate		Fourth Sunday before Easter
Caput Jejunii	Popeleční středa	First day of Lent
Cathedra Petri		22 February
Circumsision Domini	Obřezání Páně	1 January
Conception	Početí Panny Marie	9 December
Coena Domini	Zelený čtvrtek	Thursday before Easter, Maundy Thursday
Commemoration animarium	Dušičky	2 November
Conversion Pauli		25 January
Corpus Christi	Boží Tělo	Second Sunday after Pentecost
Dies Adoration	Velký Pátek	Friday before Easter
Dies Magnus	Boží Hod Veli-konoční	Easter Sunday
Epiphania Domini		6 January
Estomihi		Seventh Sunday before Easter
Eucarias		20 February
Exaudi		Sunday before Pent-acost
Exurge		Sunday before Easter
Festum Eucariste		Thursday before Easter
Indicavit		Sixth Sunday before Easter
Jubiliati		Third Sunday before Easter
Judica		Second Sunday before Easter
Laetare, Lataere		Third Sunday before Christmas
Lent		Begins on Ash Wednesday, forty days before Easter, ends on Easter Sunday
Misericordia Domini		Second Sunday after Easter
Nativitas Domini	Boží Hod Vánoční	Christmas Day
Nativitas Mariae		8 September
Oculi		Fourth Sunday before Easter
Omnium Sanctorum	Všech Svatých	1 November
Palmarum		First Sunday before Easter
Pascha, Dies Magnus	Velikonoce Boží Hod Veli-konoční	Easter Sunday

The Calendar

Latin	Czech	Date
Passio Dominica	Velký Pátek	Good Friday, Friday before Easter
Pentecoste	Svatodušní Svátky	Seventh Sunday before Easter
Purificatio Mariae		2 February
Quadragesima		Sixth Sunday before Easter
Quasimoda		Sunday before Easter
Quinquagesima		Seventh Sunday before Easter
Resurrection	Velikonoce	Easter
Rogationum		Fifth Sunday before Easter
Sabbatum Magnum	Bílá Sobota	Saturday before Easter
Sct Michaelis Arch.		20 September
Sexagesima		Eighth Sunday before Pentecost
Trinitatis		Eighth Sunday before Easter
Trium Regim		Eighth Sunday after Easter
Visitation		5 July
Vocemjucundatis		Fifth Sunday after Easter
	Stědrý den	24 December
	Vánoce	Christmas Season

Names of the Months:

Latin	Czech	German	English
Ianuarius	Leden	Januar	January
Februarius	Únor	Februar	February
Martius	Březen	Maerz	March
Aprilis	Duben	April	April
Maius	Květen or Máj	Mai	May
Iunius	Červen	Juni	June
Iulius	Červenec	Juli	July
Augustus	Srpen	August	August
September	Září	September	September
October	Říjen	Oktober	October
November	Listopad	November	November
December	Prosinec	Dezember	December

Some expressions designating the division of time:

Latin	Czech	German	English
Annus	Rok	Jahr	Year
Annus bisextus	Přestupný rok	Schaltjahr	Leap year

Latin	Czech	German	English
Mensis	Měsíc	Monat	Month
Hebdomada	Týden	Woche	Week
Ver, Origo	Jaro	Fruehling	Spring
Aestas	Léto	Sommer	Summer
Autumnus	Podzim	Herbst	Fall
Hiem	Zima	Winter	Winter
Dies	Neděle	Sonntag	Sunday
Dominicus			
Dies Lunae	Pondělí	Montag	Monday
Dies Martis	Uterý	Dienstag	Tuesday
Dies Mercurii	Středa	Mittwoch	Wednesday
Dies Jovis	Čtvrtek	Donnerstag	Thursday
Dies Veneris	Pátek	Freitag	Friday
Sabbatum	Sobota	Samstag	Saturday

There are several ways that an exact date might have been entered in the records in Czech, for example, 3 February 1850 could be written as:

3. února 1850
3. února 50 (the bar over the figure 50 indicates the current century)
3. II. 1850 (February 1850)
3. 2. 1850 (February 1850)
18 3/2 50 (3 February 1850)
Tretího února Léta Páné 1850.

As the scribes often used words instead of numerals for the days of the month, the following table might be of use to the reader (all are in their original form):

	Latin	Czech	Slovak	German
I	Primus, prima, primum	První	Prvý	Erste
II	Secondus	Druhý	Druhý	Zweite
III	Tertius	Tretí	Tretí	Dritte
IV	Quartus	Ctvrtý	Stvrtý	Vierte
V	Quintus	Páty	Piaty	Fuenfte
VI	Sextus	Šestý	Siesty	Sechste
VII	Septimus	Sedmy	Siedmy	Siebente
VIII	Octavus	Osmy	Osmy	Achte
IX	Nonus	Devátý	Deviaty	Neunte
X	Decimus	Desátý	Desiaty	Zehnte
XI	Undecimus	Jedenáctý	Jedenásty	Elfte
XII	Duodecimus	Dvanáctý	Dvanásty	Zwoelfte
XIII	Tertius Decimus	Trinácty	Trinásty	Dreizehnte
XIV	Quartus Decimus	Čtrnáctý	Strnásty	Fuerzehnte
XV	Quintus Decimus	Patnáctý	Piatnásty	Fienfzehnte
XVI	Sextus Decimus	Šestnáctý	Siestnásty	Sechzehnte
XVII	Septimus Decimus	Sedmnáctý	Siedmnásty	Siebzehnte
XVIII	Duodevicesimus	Osmnáctý	Osmnásty	Achtzehnte
XIX	Undevicesimus	Devatenáctý	Deviatnásty	Neuenzehnte

	Latin	Czech	Slovak	German
XX	Vicesimus	Dvacátý	Dvadsiaty	Zwanzigste
XXI	Vicesimus Primus	Dvacátý prvý	Dvadsiaty prvý	Ein und Zwanzigste
XXII	Vicesimus secundus	Dvacátý druhý	Dvadsiaty druhý	Zwei und Zwanzigste
XXIII	Vicesimus Testius	Dvacátý tretí	Dvadsiaty tretí	Drei und Zwanzigste
XXIV	Vicesimus Quartus	Dvacátý čtvrtý	Dvadsiaty štvrtý	Fuer und Zwanzigste
XXV	Vicesimus Quintus	Dvacátý pátý	Dvadsiaty piaty	Fuenf und Zwanzigste
XXVI	Vicesimus Sextus	Dvacátý šestý	Dyadsiaty šiesty	Sechs und Zwanzigste
XVII	Vicesimus Septimus	Dvacátý sedmý	Dvadsiaty siedmy	Sieben Zwanzigste
XXVIII	Duodetricesimus	Dvacátý osmý	Dvadsiaty osmy	Acht und Zwanzigste
XXIX	Undetricesimus	Dvacátý devátý	Dvadsiaty deviaty	Neun und Zwanzigste
XXX	Tricesimus	Tricáty	Tridsiaty	Dreisigste
XXXI	Tricesimus Primus	Tricáty první	Tridsiaty prvý	Ein und Dreisigste

BIBLIOGRAPHY

Bennett, Archibald F. A GUIDE FOR GENEALOGICAL RESEARCH. Salt Lake City: Genealogical Society of the Church of Jesus Christ of Latter-Day Saints, 1951. GL 929.1 B439g.

The appendix contains many valuable tables and lists; one of them is the Latin equivalents of the numerals.

Emler, Joseph. RUKOVĚŤ CHRONOLOGIE KŘESTANSKÉ, ZVLÁŠTĚ ČESKÉ. Prague: Historický spolek, 1876.

It is a handbook of Christian chronology for the years 800 to 2000 A.D.

Sedlák, V.J. TABULKY K PŘEVÁDĚNÍ DAT HISTORICKÝCH PRAMENŮ. Prague: Genealogická a heraldická společnost, 1970. GL 943.7 Al no 2 or Microfilm 845,441 (5th item).

Tables for interpreting the dates of historical events.

Chapter 9

LANGUAGE

No two Slavic languages are so much alike as Czech and Slovak. The similarity applies to vocabulary, sentence structure, grammatical constructions and expressions. However, the differences in the two languages are still such that knowledge of both Czech and Slovak is necessary to do genealogical research in both Bohemian lands and Slovakia. To aid the researcher, some excellent textbooks and dictionaries have been listed in the bibliography of this chapter.

In its development, the Czech language has been influenced by both German and Latin. The German influence was strong because of political and geographical proximity; but, with the growth of the Catholic church, Latin became the language of documents. Not only have many Latin words been assimilated into spoken Czech, but the structure of Czech grammar has also been affected. In spite of these foreign influences, however, the native language was spoken with pride and some major literary works have been written in Czech.

The spelling of words was progressively simplified, until the Czech language differed greatly from other Slavic languages, including Slovak. The diacritical marks above the vowels ('slash' čárka and 'hook' háček) and also above some consonants (háček) replaced the composite spellings that produced the same sounds; for example, in Polish cz for Czech c and sz for s. In Czech only one letter is used for a sound.

Czech is considered one of the most difficult languages to learn. I do not recommend studying it without an instructor and a good dictionary. The glossaries, alphabet, lists of occupations, numerals, and names included in this book should be of help to the genealogical researcher, but caution should be exercised in their use. The principal stumbling block in reading the Czech matriky and documents is the grammar. Since this is not a grammar book, only those aspects of grammar which are most important for understanding genealogical sources will be included. The declension of names and adjectives and the past tense of verbs will be discussed. It is impossible to list all grammatical deviations which could change the meaning of the entry in the matriky or in other documents, but those that follow should help the researcher.

The given names and surnames, listed in the chapter "Names," appear in the nominative case (the subject of the sentence). In English the name does not decline according to its position in the sentence. The Czech name, however, has seven grammatical cases. A working knowledge of only six of the cases is necessary for genealogical purposes. The vocative (the fifth case) as direct form of address does not appear in the matriky or in the old documents. To make the list easily comprehensible, only the phrases most frequently used in the matriky and old documents, which require a name to be used in one of the grammatical cases, will be given. The declension of a name requires certain changes be made in its ending. The name Václav Bednář will be used because it illustrates both a "hard" (Václav) and "soft" (Bednář) declension pattern.

Nominative: Václav Bednář oženil se (Václav Bednář was married)

Genitive: Marie, dcera Václava Bednáře (Marie, daughter of Václav Bednář)

Dative: Marie věnovala Václavu Bednáři, or Bednárovi (Marie endowed Václav Bednář)

Accusative: Marie si vzala Václava Bednáře (Marie married Václav Bednář)

Locative: Marie zdědila po Václavu Bednáři, or Bednárovi (Marie inherited from Václav Bednář)

Instrumental: Karel Hájek s Václavem Bednářem (Karel Hájek with Václav Bednář)

Feminine names in Czech experience a similar metamorphosis. The majority of feminine given names end in an -a, though some end in -ie (Merie, Žofie). Feminine surnames, on the other hand, are derived from their masculine counterparts by adding the ending -ová.

Nominative: Anna (Marie) Sedláková se narodila (Anna Sedláková was born)

Genitive: Jan, syn Anny (Marie) Sedlákové (Jan, son of Anna Sedláková)

Dative: Jan věnoval Anně (Marii) Sedlákové (Jan endowed Anna Sedláková)

Accusative: Jan si vzal Annu (Marii) Sedlákovou (Jan
                 married Anna Sedláková)

Locative: Jan zdědil po Anně (Marii) Sedlákové (Jan
                 inherited from Anna Sedláková)

Instrumental: Jan se oženil s Annou (Marii) Sedlákovou
                 (Jan married with Anna Sedláková)

Adjectives also appear in masculine, feminine and neuter
forms. However, the neuter adjectives are not discussed
here because they seldom appear in the matriky or old documents. Like the nouns (names), the adjectives also decline
in seven cases.

	Male	Female
Nominative	Bohatý (rich)	Bohatá
Genitive	Bohatého	Bohaté
Dative	Bohatému	Bohaté
Accusative	Bohatého	Bohatou
Locative	Bohatém	Bohaté
Instrumental	Bohatým	Bohatou

There are some adjectives which have the ending -i in both
genders. The declension, however, is different:

	Male	Female
Nominative	Místní (local)	Místní
Genitive	Místního	Místní
Dative	Místnímu	Místní
Accusative	Místního	Místní
Locative	Místním	Místní
Instrumental	Místním	Místní

There are numerous grammatical rulings concerning Czech
verbs. Only two will be discussed here. Dictionaries
list the verbs in their infinitive form (dělati--to do).
However, the old documents and matriky usually use only
the past tense (the few verbs listed in the glossary are
in this form). The following table might be useful to
those who search through the old records:

Infinitive form:	Past Tense: Male:	Female
Býti (to be)	Byl	Byla
Vzíti si (to take a spouse)	Vzal si	Vzala si
Oženiti se (to marry)	Oženil se	Provdala se
Naroditi se (to be born)	Narodil se	Narodila se

	Past Tense:	
Infinitive form:	Male:	Female:
Zemříti (to die)	Zemřel	Zemřela

These are some of the most important items to be aware of
when searching Czech records; additional deviations from
the nominatives of the nouns and infinitives of the verbs
should be checked in any of the recommended Czech textbooks. Fortunately, the language used in the matriky is
very repetitious, so that once the researcher has unraveled
the meaning of one entry, he will be able to understand
most of the entries.

Unless one falls heir to some old family letters, dialects
will not represent a problem in Czech genealogical research.
The matriky and old records are usually in the central dialect of the České Země and in the central dialect of Slovakia. The following are the dialects spoken in the various
parts of the republic:

Bohemian 1- The central dialect with Prague as its focus.
            This dialect also forms the basis of modern
            literary Czech.
          2- The northeastern dialect, spoken northeast
            of Prague.
          3- The southwestern dialect, spoken southwest
            of Prague.

Moravian, Silesian:
          1- The Hanák dialect, centered around Brno and
            Prostějov.
          2- The Lach dialect of Silesia, which forms a
            transition to Polish and reminds one also of
            the Eastern Slovakian dialect.

Slovakian: (each of these dialects is subdivided into num-
            erous subdialects):
          1- Central Slovak dialects, used as the literary
            language of Slovaks. Certain features of
            these dialects bring them close to the
            Moravian dialect of Czech and, at the same
            time, form a transition to Polish.
          2- Western Slovakian dialect (this is now the
            second official language of the Czechoslovak
            republic. See chapter on history.)
          3- Eastern Slovakian. This dialect bears a strong
            resemblance to Polish and Ukrainian.

Once again the reader must be cautioned that mastering
some of the rules and words in this chapter will not be
sufficient for interpreting entries in the matriky and old
records with foolproof accuracy. To avoid errors, it is
recommended that the researcher copy each entry, including

the family surname, exactly the way he sees it. The interpretation and evaluation can be done later, preferably
with the help of someone who is thoroughly familiar with
the language. Many reports of archivists in Czechoslovakia
are prepared in just such a manner. First, list the details
concerning the book where the entry was found; then quote
the entry verbatim, including the possible errors in spelling of the names or of the grammar of the language. (See
samples following the chapter on sources). Overall, it is
more efficient to engage a Czech native to help with the
translation and interpretation, than to risk making an error
which would result in hours of futile research. The Genealogical Library has a list of competent, accredited genealogists who can be employed by individuals researching their
family names.

We now come to the task of reading the difficult handwriting.
As explained in the chapter on sources, very few genealogical records extend further back than the beginning of the
seventeenth century. The handwriting used in documents
prior to this time, therefore, does not concern the genealogical researcher. The majority of the documents preserved before 1620 have been added to the holdings of the
archives, classified, and, in some cases, rewritten according to modern convention. The handwriting of the pre-
seventeenth century papers resembles very much that used
in England, called the Gothic. In some instances, the
modified version of this writing remained in use till about
1650.

With the fall of the České Země to the Hapsburgs in 1620,
the Germanizing influence in the nation was strongly felt
in every phase of public life. The priests were ordered
to keep their matriky either in German or Latin. Their
protests were to no avail. Latin sometimes caused a drastic change in the spelling of names but it is not much
different from the written Latin of today.

Some priests struck a compromise by using German script
while keeping the text itself in Czech. This practice was
popularly called Švabach and was used by the priests,
public scribes, schools or individuals till the late
nineteenth century. Following this chapter is a table
listing the German alphabet along with some samples of its
use. Pure German script is incompatible with writing in
the Czech language, which resulted in some curious adjustments. The typically Czech accent mark over vowels (Sladký), which indicate that they should be pronounced with a
long sound, have been replaced by the German "umlaut"--
double dots above the letter (Sladký). The soft pronounciation of š (sh) has been indicated by a double s
(Ssladký). The soft sound ž retained its marking as did
the ř, although in some instances the latter was spelled
rz (Jirzi). The letter f was often doubled (Joseff). The

Czech j is found in švabach as g (mag--maj, gegj--její),
or y (vejr). The i was often spelled as j (gegj--její).
The frequent appearance of the Czech sound ou is found in
švabach as au (surnames: Auředníček--Ouředníček; Saudek--
Soudek). Names beginning with the letter o have been preceded by the letter v (Obora--Vobora; Otrok--Votrok).
Following this chapter is a table which gives some help in
deciphering the švabach writing, listing letters which
reach above the line, letters limited to the middle line,
letters extending below the line, and finally, letters that
extend both above and below the line. These charts may be
of assistance in reading the records in švabach.

However, not all the matriky from the beginning of the
seventeenth till the end of the nineteenth century were
written in Gothic, švabach, or German. There were some
parishes where the ministers consistently maintained their
native customs and writing. Surprisingly, this occurred not
only in big cities, where one would expect the clergy to
be more nationalistic, but also in small villages. Unfortunately, one can never predict which way the books were
kept and in which language. The language often changed
from one priest, or his clerk, to another, sometimes from
page to page.

Some of the matriky or other records of genealogical value
might have been kept in "modern writing" as early as 1800.
Since then the people in Czechoslovakia have used the present-day script, which differs only slightly from that used
in other countries. Although penmanship has been an important subject in schools, handwriting, unfortunately, has
always followed the individual vagaries of the penman with
the writing of some slanting to the right, some to the left
and some rigidly straight standing. In the last century,
a vogue developed for a certain flair in handwriting,
especially for capital letters. As there was no limit to
the form nor the imagination of the writers performing
such pen and paper feats, it is difficult to read such
first letters; one often has to read the whole word first,
and from the context then determine the first letter.

Czech-American families might be in possession of old
letters, passports, or other old documents written in
Czech. How wonderful it would be if they could read these
valuable possessions; and, with the aid of a dictionary,
render them into English! Unfortunately, many cannot even
read the writing, which is often full of grammatical and
other errors (in old letters), or sloppy script (in old
documents). Fortunately, in modern writing there are very
few differences between English and Czech; a sample list
of the most pronounced differences that may appear in the
letters or documents of recent years follows in Tables B
and C.

Letters written on the line:

m - a ; *c* - c ; *v* - e;
i - i ; *m* - m ; *n* - n;
o - o ; *r* - r ; *w* - w;
v - v ; *w* - w

Letters extending above the line:

b - b ; *d* - d ; *k* - k
l - l ; *t* - t

Letters extending below the line:

g - g ; *j* - j ; *p* - p;

y - y ; *z* - z

Letters extending above and below the line:

f - f ; *h* - h ; *s* - s

Table A
German Script

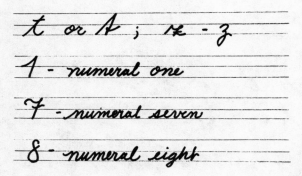

Table B

Samples of Differences between Modern Writing
in Czechoslovakia and the United States

Table C

CESKA ABECEDA
(CZECH ALPHABET)

The following is the order of the Czech alphabet as it is
found in indexes to books and postal guides or in alphabetical listings of names. For the convenience of English-
speaking readers, this order has not been followed in this
book. There are three accent markings in Czech language:
/ (čárka--'slash') indicating that the vowel should be
pronounced with a long sound--see examples in the alphabet;
✓ (háček--'checkmark') indicating that the vowel or consonant should be pronounced softly; ° (krouzek--'circle'),
used only above the letter u, indicating that it should be
pronounced with a long sound. There are no native words
containing letters "Q," "X," and "W." These are used only
in foreign names and words. Their pronounciation is indicated in the alphabet. There is no equivalent in Czech for
the English sound "th"; words containing this sound are pronounced with a "d" (that--dat).

	Sample Czech word	Sample English word
a	Anna	utmost
á	Václav	far
b	Boleslav	bread
c	Cyril	cats
č	Čech	chin
ď	ďábel	dew
e	Eva	let
é	malé	hand
ě	běda	Vietnam
f	Filip	Philip
g	Olga	Olga
h	Havel	hand
ch	Chrudoš	loch
i	Ignac	give
í	Hermína	bee
j	Jan	yes

122

	Sample Czech word	Sample English word
k	Karel	ma<u>k</u>e
l	Lazar	<u>l</u>eft
m	Martin	<u>m</u>other
n	Nepomuk	<u>n</u>othing
o	Oskar	Cl<u>o</u>tilda
ó	móda	<u>fo</u>r
p	Pavel	<u>p</u>art
q	Kvído	<u>kv</u>
r	Rádek	<u>rar</u>e
ř	Rehoř	<u>rz</u>
s	Samuel	<u>S</u>amuel
š	Šárka	<u>sh</u>ort
t	Tomáš	<u>t</u>wo
ť	Taťána	<u>t</u>une
u	Urban	p<u>u</u>t
ú	útěk	b<u>oo</u>t
ů	dům	b<u>oo</u>t
v	Václav	<u>v</u>endor
w	pronounced as v - (we - ve)	
x	Zsantipa	<u>K</u>santipa
y	Yvona	b<u>i</u>t
ý	malý	m<u>ee</u>t
z	Zuzana	<u>z</u>enith
ž	Žofie	plea<u>s</u>ure

The Slovak alphabet reads much the same as the Czech alphabet. The letters "<u>Q</u>," "<u>W</u>," and "<u>X</u>" appear only in foreign words. However, the following Czech letters do not appear in the Slovak language: "<u>Ě</u>," "<u>Ř</u>," and "<u>Ů</u>." "<u>Ě</u>" is spelled as <u>ie</u> and pronounced the same. In Slovak there are three

types of letter "<u>L</u>": "<u>L</u>" as in Czech; "<u>L</u>"--a long sound
made with the tongue rolled back somewhat; and an "<u>L</u>" pronounced softly as in "million."

ABBREVIATIONS (ZKRATKY) FREQUENTLY USED IN BOOKS AND DOCUMENTS

Abbreviation	Latin	Czech	English
AD	Anno Domini	Léta Páně	The year of our Lord
aet.	Aetatis	ve věku	in the age of
Ai	Anni	roku	in the year
al.	Alias	jinak	alias
ao	Anno	roku	in the year
A.S.N.	Anno Salvatoria Nostri	roku Spasitele našeho	year of our Savior
bapt.	baptizatus	pokřtěný	christened
b.m.	Baetae Memoriae	blahé paměti	blessed memory
cca	circa	asi	about
cf	confer	srovnej	compare
cop.vid.	copia vidimata	ověřený opis	certified copy
c.p.	cum pertinentiis	s příslušen-stvím	with all belongings
def.	defunctus	zemřelý	deceased
den.	denatus	zemřelý	deceased
dnus	dominus	Pán	Lord
dto	detto	totéž	ditto
ed.	editid	vydal	issued by
em.	emeritus	vysloužilý	emeritus
fec.	fecit	udělal	made
fl. or fr.	florenus	zlatý	gold piece

Abbreviation	Latin	Czech	English
fol.	folium	list, stránka	page
gdh.	(see glossary)	gruntovní kniha	land book
gen.	generosus	urozený	nobly born
gr.alb.		groš bílý	white coin
h.a.	huius anni	tohoto roku	this year
hon.	honestus	počestný	honest
hum.	humatus	pohřben	buried
ib.	ibidem	tamtéž	ibid.
i.f.	ipse fecit	sám učinil	did himself
inc.	incertus	nejistý	uncertain
J.M.C.		Jeho císařská milost	His Imperial Majesty
Kr.		krejcar	coin of the smallest value
l.c.	loco citato	na uvedeném místě	at the mentioned place
M.Mag.	Magister	mistr	master
mort.	mortuus	zemřelý	deceased
m.p.	manu propria	vlastnoruční podpis	own signature
nat.	natus	narozený	born
neb.	sepultus	nebožtík	deceased
N.N.	nomec nescio	jméno neznámé	name not known
ob.	obit	zemřel	died
pag. or pg.	pagina	stránka	page
par.	parochia	fara	parish
P.B.V.		Pán Bůh Všemohoucí	Almighty God

Abbreviation	Latin	Czech	English
praen.d.	praenobilis dominus	urozený pán	well-born lord
p.t.	pleno titulo	plným titulem	full title
p.v.	pagina versa	zadní strana listu	reverse side of the document
rel.	relictus	pozůstalý	relict
ren.	renatus	pokřtěný	christened
sep.	sepultus	pohřbený	buried
SS		zaopatřen svátostmi	received the last rites
tum.	tumultus	pohřben	buried
u.s.	ut supra	jako výše	as above
vol.	volumen	svazek	volume

GLOSSARY

The following is not an exhaustive vocabulary but rather
a listing of terms often used in genealogical, heraldic,
and historical sources. A brief translation or clarifica-
tion of the terms is included. An "L" indicates Latin
derivation.

A

Abavia L	Second great-grandmother
Abavus L	Second great-grandfather
Abortivus L	Born prematurely
Acatholicus L	Non-Catholic
Adolescens L	Young man
Adulterium L	Adultery. See Cizoložství
Aetas L	Age. See Stáří
Affinitas L	Relative-in-law
Agnatus L	Male line of ancestors. See Po meči

An, Anno L	Year
Anita L	Aunt. See Teta
Annus Bissextus L	Leap year. See Přestupný rok
Anti L	Before. See Před
Asi	About. See Circa
Avi L	Ancestor. See Patres, Předek
Avia L	Grandmother. See Bába
Avunculus L	Uncle, mother's brother. See Patruus, Strýc
Avus L	Grandfather. See Děd

B

Bába, also babička	Grandmother (Great-grandmother--prababa). See Avia
Baptisatus L	Christened. See Krtěn
Bastard L	Illegitimate child. See Děti
Blíženci	Twins. See Dvajčata, Frater Germanus, Gemellae, and Gemelli
Bratr	Brother. See Frater Germanus
Bratranec	Male cousin. See Gener
Bratrská Jednota	Protestant religious society which originated during the reign of Jiří Poděbradský (fifteenth century) from among the ranks of the followers of Jan Hus. Sometimes also called Pod Obojí, meaning that they partook of both forms of the sacrament--bread and wine. They were greatly influenced by the peasant philosopher, Petr Chelčický.
Brezen	March

C

Cappellanus L	Chaplain. See Kaplan
Celo-láník	A farmer who owned a whole lán (a metric measure). See Sedlák
Červen	June

Červenec	July
České Země	Czech lands (Bohemia, Moravia, Silesia)
Chalupník	Owner of a cottage with a small plot for a garden. See Domkář, Sedlák, Zahradník
Chelčický, Petr	See Bratrská Jednota
Chronogram	Calendar
Cippus L	Gravestone. See Náhrobek
Circa L	About. See Asi
Církev	Church (an institution, not a building)
Civic (civ.) L	Citizen. See Občan
Cizinec	Traveler. See Peregrinus
Cizoložství	Adultery. See Adulterium
V cizoložství zplozené	Children. See Děti
Clericus	Minister, priest. See Duchovní
Člověčenství	An oath of loyalty and obedience by the vassal to the overlord. See Poddanství
Coelebes L	Unmarried, single
Coemeterium L	Cemetery. See Hřbitov
Cognatio L	Female line of ancestors. See Po preslici
Commater L	Godmother. See Kmotra
Compater L	Godfather. See Kmotr
Conjux L	Husband and wife, married couple
Copulation L	Marriage ceremony. ·See Solemmicatio, Svadba
Čtvrt - láník	Farmer who owned one fourth of a lán. See Sedlák

D

Dcera	Daughter. See Puera

Děd — Grandfather (great-grandfather--praděd)
See Avus

Dědic — Heir. See Heres

Dědička — Heiress

Děti, dítky — Children (See each term in its alphabetical order)
Filiace--basic family unit of father, mother, and child
Vlastní, rodné or plnorodné--parents' own children
Nevlastní--step-children
Poloviční po otci--when father is one's own
Poloviční po matce (also životní)--when mother is one's own
Zákonné, manželské, řádné zplozené--of married parents
Nemanželský, Nezákonné, přirozené, neřádně zplozené, nepravé, levoboček, bastard, parchant, v cizoložství zplozené, spratek--illegitimate children

Dívčí jméno — Maiden name. See Olin

Domkář — Owner of a cottage with a small plot for a garden. See Chalupník, Sedlák, Zahradník

D.S.P. L — Died without issue

Duchovní — Minister, priest. See Clericus

Dvajčata — Twins

D. vita matria L — Died while mother was living

D. vita patria L — Died while father was living

E

Ecclesia L — Church

Erb — Coat of arms. See Znak

Exulant — Forced exile; applies mainly to the conditions following 1620 with the fall of the Czech lands to the Hapsburgs

F

Familiant — See Sedlák

Familiaris L	Relative
Fara	Parish. See Paroch
Farní obvod, F.o.	Abbreviation used mainly in the Guides to the Archival Collections, meaning villages, settlements or hamlets under the jurisdiction of a parish. See chapter on "Archives"
Filiace	Basic family unit of father, mother, and children. See Děti
Filiaster L	Stepson, son-in-law. See Nevlastní
Fojt	Overseer of a feudal estate, a marshal
Frater L	Brother. See Bratr
Frater Germanus L	Twin brother

G

Gemellae L	Female twins
Gemelli L	Twins. See Blíženci, Dvajčata
Gener L	Male cousin. See Bratranec, Zeť
Generace	Generation. See Pokolení
Genetica	Physical qualities or character traits inherited from the ancestry
Genitores L	Parents. See Parentus, Rodiče
Gens L	Male line
Genus L	Gender. See Pohlaví
Germanus L (Germana)	Brother (sister). See Bratr, Sestra, Soror, Sororius
Glejt	Document of safe conduct, passport (used before 1620); required, but not always respected. See List průvodní, List železný
Grunt	Family property (old expression)
Gruntovní knihy	Land records. See Urbář. See chapter on "Sources for Genealogical Research in Czechoslovakia"
Gubernium	From 1763 to 1848, the highest administrative office in Prague and Brno

H

Heraldika	Heraldry
Heres L	Heir. See Dědic
Hlavní rodová linie	Direct line following the father's ancestry
Homicidium L	Murder. See Vražda
Hrad	In the Middle Ages the residence of the ruler or nobility. The resident had administrative rights for the vicinity. Clans living in the hrad often took the name of the hrad as their surname, or vice versa--the hrad receiving its name from the resident family. The hrad was surrounded by protective walls. Later it lost its military importance and the family lived in the more comfortable zámky (see Zámek). The lesser nobility occupied a well-protected residence called a tvrz. See Tvrz
Hřbitov	Cemetery. See Coemeterium
Humatus (Humata) L	Buried. See Pohřben, S.U.P., Sepultus, Tumulatus

I

Ignotus L	Unknown
Impraegnata L	Pregnant before marriage
Incertus L	Uncertain
Incolatus L	Citizenship, residence, domicile; aliens in permanent residence without having citizenship
Infans L	Infant
Inkolát	Naturalization. Included the oath and signing of an obligation whereby the applicant accepted the responsibility of a citizen and recognized the Czech king as his only ruler. The practice was discontinued in 1848.

J

Jaro, na jaře	Spring, in spring
Jedináček	Only child

Jednota Bratrská	Pod Obojí, Chelčicky Petr, Unitas Fratrum. See Bratrská Jednota
Jesse	Savior's Pedigree. Often found on the title page of the matriky. It has the form of a tree, growing out of the bosom of David's father, Jesse. The branches contain pictures of Christ's main ancestors. In the crown of the tree there is the likeness of Jesus and his mother, Mary.
Jméno	Name. Usually means both given name and surname. See Nomen
Josefinský katastr	See Katastr
Juvenis L	Young man, bachelor

K

Kalendář	Calendar
Kaplan	Chaplain. See Cappellanus
Katastr	Census of the heads of families, listing the location of the land owned by the family. Prepared for the assessment of taxes
Kmotr	See Compater
Kmotra	Godmother. See Commater
Kmotři	Godparents. See Levans
Kněz	Priest. See Clericus, Duchovní, Parochus, Plebanus, Reverendus, Sacordos
Kognát	Female line of ancestors. See Cognatio
Kompaktáty	Documents listing conditions of the peace between the Hussites and the Roman Catholic Church, 1436
Kraj	District, area
Krajský soud	County court of law. See Soud
Kronika obecní	An account of happenings kept either daily or occasionally by the local recorder
Kronika rodinná	An account of births, marriages, and deaths kept by someone in the family, usually on the blank pages of the Bible

Křtěn, křtěna	Christened. The "a" ending indicates the feminine gender. See Baptisatus
Kšaft	Testament. Archaic expression meaning last will. See Poslední vůle
Kvartery	Records of procedures under the highest court in Bohemia and Moravia. See Zemské desky
Květen	May

L

Lán	A metrical measure. See Sedlák
Leden	January
Leník	Recipient of léno. See Man, Léno
Léno	Land and/or privileges given by the king or the local nobility to a leník (vassal) under certain conditions and oath of loyalty. See Leník, Man
Léta Páně	The year of our Lord.
Léto, v létě	Summer, in summer
Letopočet	The date
Levans L	Godparents. See Kmotři
Levoboček	Illegitimate child. See Děti
Z levého boku	Literal translation "from the left hip," refers to an illegitimate child
Liber rusticus L	Free peasant
Ligatus L	Husband. See Manžel, Muž
List	Document
List bílý	Carte blanche
List cechovní	Document of the mastery of a trade
List dílčí	Agreement on the division of property
List erbovní	Document granting a coat of arms
List fedrovní	Document listing an individual's employment record
Listina	Legal document

List kšaftovni	Testament. See Kšaft, Poslední vůle
Listopad	November
List průvodní	See Glejt
List řádného na svět zplození	Document verifying a legitimate birth
List věnný	Agreement on the bride's dowry
List železný	See Glejt

M

Macecha	Stepmother
Majestát	Grant of freedom, privilege or land usually bestowed by kings
Man	Recipient of léno. See Leník, Léno
Manu propria (m.n.) L	Signed personally
Manžel	Husband. See Ligatus, Muž
Manželé	Married couple. See Mariti
Manželka	Wife. See Marita, Žena
Manželské děti	Of married parents. See Děti
Manželství	Matrimony. See Matrimonium
Marita L	Wife. See Manželka
Mariti L	Married couple. See Manželé
Mater L	Mother. See Matka
Mater Meretrix L	Illegitimate mother
Matertera L	Mother's sister. See Teta
Matka	Mother. See Mater
Matrika, matriky	Parish register (matriky indicates plural); includes records pertaining to individuals used by schools, members of the military, records of nobility, and other organizations
Matrimonium L	Matrimony. See Manželství

Matrina, Materna L   Godmother. See Commater, Kmotra

Měštan   Burgher, citizen of a city; privilege
                     gained either by inheritance or by pay-
                     ing a sum of money. Lists of such citi-
                     zens, at various times, were deposited
                     in the city halls

Měštanka   Female version of the preceding. See
                     Měštan

More novo (m.n.) L   New reckoning, new style of data. See
                     chapter on "Calendar"

More vetere   Old reckoning, old style of data. See
   (m.v.) L   chapter on "Calendar"

Mors, Mortia L   Death. See Úmrtí, Zesnutí

Muž   Husband. See Ligatus, Manžel

N

Náhrobek   Gravestone. See Cippus

Nájemce   Tenant. See Pachtýř

Narozen(a)   Born. See Natus. The letter "a" indi-
                     cates female gender

Narození   Birth

Natus L   See Narozen

Neděle   Sunday

Nemanželský,   See Děti
   nemanželská

Nemocný, nemocná   Sick, ill

Nepos, Nepus L   Grandchild, nephew, descendant. See
                     Patruelis, Potomstvo, Synovec, Vnouce

Nepravé Děti   Illegitimate child. See Děti

Neptis L   Granddaughter, niece, descendant. See
                     Neteř, Potomstvo, Vnučka

Neřadně zplozené   Illegitimate child. See Děti
   děti

Neteř   Niece. See Neptis

Nevěsta   Bride

Nevlastní	Stepchildren. See Děti
Nevolnictví	Vassal obligations to the overlord. See Poddanství, Robota, Vyvázení
Nevolník	Vassal. See Poddanství
Nezákonné Děti	Illegitimate child. See Děti
Nobilitace	Awarding a title of nobility
Nomen	See Jméno
Notářství	A county office, established 20 September 1850 and discontinued in 1960. Its purpose was to prepare public papers, wedding contracts, and last wills. The files of the retiring or deceased notary were sealed and deposited at the county court. State archives now contain papers of the notaries 1850-1960. See chapter on "Archives"
Nuptiae L	Wedding. See Oddavky, Sňatek
Nurus	Daughter-in-law. See Snacha

O

Občan	Citizen. See Civic
Obiit repentina Morte L	Died without sacrament, suddenly
Oblast	District
Obsequia L	Funeral. See Pohřeb
Oddavky	Wedding. See Nuptiae, Sňatek
Odpočívej v pokoji	Rest in peace. See Requiescat in pace
Okresní soud	County court. Important for genealogists, since it houses papers and documents of orphans' cases. See Soud, Krajský soud, Zemsky soud
Olin L	See Dívčí jméno
Orbus, orba, orphanus L	Orphan. See Sirotek
Osvojený(á)	Adopted. The letter "a" indicates female gender.

Otčím	Stepfather
Otec	Father. See Pater

P

Pachtýř	Tenant. See Nájemce
Pagina L (p., pag.)	Page. See Stránka
Panna	Virgin. See Puella, Virgo
Parchant	Bastard. This term appears in the parish registers and is meant to be rather derogatory. See Děti
Parentus L (p., par.)	Parents. See Rodiče, Genitores
Paroch L	Parish. See Fara
Parochus L	Priest. See Clericus, Duchovní, Kněz, Plebanus, Reverendus, Sacordos
Pastor	Stepson
Pastorkyně	Stepdaughter
Pátek	Friday
Pater L	Father. See Otec
Patres L	Forefather. See Avus, Předek
Patrimoniální sprava	Summary of the political and legal rights and the rights of taxation which the feudal lords had over the vassal. Used only to 1848
Patruelis L	Descendant. See Nepos, Synovec
Patruus L	Uncle, mother's brother. See Avunculus, Strýc
Peregrinus L	Traveler. See Cizinec
Plebanie L	Limits or jurisdiction of the parish
Plebanus L	Priest. See Clericus, Duchovní, Kněz, Parochus, Reverendus, Sacordos
Plnorodné děti	Parents' own children. See Děti

Poddanství	The established relationship between the owner of the estate or member of the privileged class and the persons dependent on him. Poddanství was discontinued in 1848
	Nevolnictví (poddanství, vassal arrangement) was so restrictive that the vassal (nevolník) could not change his occupation, address, or the way of life of his family without the permission of the overlord. Nevolnictví was abolished by the patent of Joseph II in 1781. Člověčenstvi was an oath of loyalty and obedience by the vassal to the overlord. Vyhost was the permission given to the vassal to move into another area. See Robota, Nevolnictví, Vyvázení
Poděbradský, Jiří	Religious society which originated during the reign of Jiří Poděbradský (fifteenth century) from among the ranks of the followers of Jan Hus. See Bratrská Jednota
Podluží	Oldest land measure used in the records. It denotes the measure of the land that could be cultivated by a team of oxen or one horse
Pod Obojí	Another name for the followers of Jan Hus who belonged to the religious society Bratrská Jednota. The words "pod obojí" mean that they partook of both forms of the sacrament--bread and wine. See Bratrská Jednota
Podruh	Farm laborer who did not own any property. See Sedlak
Podsedek	Used primarily in Příbram area; often refers to unkept cottages whose owners were not city citizens and consequently did not have the rights of a měštan. See also Sedlak
Podzim, na podzim	Fall, in the fall
Pohlaví	See Genus
Pohřben(a)	Buried. See Humatus, Sepultus, S.U.P., Tumulatus. The letter "a" indicates female gender
Pohřeb	Funeral. See Obsequia

Pohrobek	Child, born after father's death; usually applied only to the sons
Pokolení	See Generace
Pokrevenci	Blood relatives
Pokrevenství	Relationship of the descendants of one or both common parents
Poloviční po otci, matce	When father is one's own. See Děti
Po meči	Male line of ancestors. See Agnatus
Pondělí	Monday
Popillus L	Motherless
Po přeslici	Female line of ancestors. See Cognatio
Popula, populi L	Illegitimate
Posledek	Last child
Poslední vůle	Testament. See Kšaft
Posteri L	Descendant. See Nepos, Neptis, Potomstvo
Posteritas L	Descendancy
Potomstvo	Nephew, descendant. See Nepos, Neptis, Posteri
Povolání	Occupation
Prabába (prababička)	Term denoting the direct ancestress. Although it is correct, one would call the ancestress personally known to him "babička." See Bába
Praděd	Great-grandfather. See Děd
Praematurum concubitus L	Illegal cohabitation
Pramáti	An expression used to indicate ancestress in general. Ofen applied to Eve, or important, well-loved royalty
Před	Before. See Anti
Predek	Forefather. See Avus, Patres
Přes pole	Literally "over the field." As used in the matriky, it means that the bride came from another village

Přestupný rok	Leap year. See Annus Bissextus
Příbuzenství	Relationship
Příbuzný	Relative. See Familiaris
Příjmení	Surname
Přirozené dítě	Illegitimate child. See Děti
Privignus L	Stepson from former marriage
Přiženil se	The bridegroom received part of his father-in-law's property
Proavia L	Great-grandmother. See Bába
Proavus L	Great-grandfather. See Děd
Proles spuria L	Illegitimate descendant
Promulgation L	Wedding announcement. See Svatební oznámení
Pronepos L	Great-grandson
Prosinec	December
Prvorozený	First-born
Puella L	Virgin. See Panna, Virgo
Puer L	Son. See Syn
Puera L	Daughter. See Dcera
Půhon	Summons
Půl láník	Farmer who owned half of the land. See Sedlák

R

Řádné zplozené	Of married parents. See Děti
Regest	An extract from a document
Rejstřík	Index
Relicta L	Widow. See Vdova
Remeslo	Trade
Renatus, Renata L	Christened. See Křten

Requiescat in pace (r.i.p.) L	Rest in peace. See Odpočívej v pokoji
Reverendus L	Priest. See Duchovní, Clericus, Kněz, Parochus, Plebanus, Sacordos
Říjen	October
Robota	Various labors the vassals had to perform for their feudal lords without pay. In 1680 the kinds and extent of these services were defined in Bohemia; and in Moravia, in 1713. The limit of the labor was three days a week. In 1775 these services were increased according to the amounts the vassals paid in taxes. Forced labor was discontinued in 1848. See also Poddanství, Nevolnictvi, Vyvazeni
Rod	All descendants or relatives of a common ancestor. Clan
Rodič, rodec, roditel	Father. Not frequently used
Rodiče	Parents. See Genitores, Parentus
Rodička, roditelka	Mother. Not frequently used
Rodina	Family
Rodné děti	Parents' own children. See Děti
Rodný list	Birth certificate
Rodopis	Genealogy
Rodopisec	Genealogist
Rodové katastry	See Katastr
Rozrod	Records of all descendants of a common ancestor
Rytíř	Knight. Member of lower nobility. His principal purpose was to wage wars, usually on horseback. He was also supposed to be a model Christian

S

Sacordos L	Priest. See Clericus, Duchovní, Kněz, Parochus, Plebanus, Reverendus

Sběhl	Willfully left the estate without the permission of the owner
Sedlák	Farmer. Also called familiant. Applied to agriculturists working on their own fields or leasing to vassals. Celo-laník--farmer who owned a whole lán Půl-laník--farmer who owned half of the lán Čtvrt-laník--farmer who owned one fourth of a lán Lán--a metrical measure Chalupník, domkář, zahradník--owner of a cottage with small plot for a garden Podruh--farm laborer who did not own any property Podsedek--laborer who leased a small field from a sedlák Svobodník--a free farmer not obligated to work as a vassal Zeman--ancient Czech word for svobodník
Sepultus	Buried. See Humatus, S.U.P., Pohřben, Tumulatus
Sestra	Sister. See Germana, Soror
Sestřenice	Female cousin
Sirotek	Orphan. See Orbus
Snacha	See Nurus
Snátek	Wedding. See Nuptiae, Oddavky
Sobota	Saturday
Socer L	Father-in-law
Socrinus L	Brother-in-law
Socrus L	Mother-in-law
Solemmicatio L	See Copulation, Svadba
Soror L	Sister. See Germana, Sestra
Sororius L	Brother-in-law
Soud	Court of law (Okresní--county; Kraj--district; Zemský--federal)
Spratek	Illegitimate child. See Děti
Spurius, spuria L	Illegitimate son, daughter

Srpen	August
Stárí	Age. See Aetas
Stirps L	Kinship
Stránka	Page. See Pagina
Středa	Wednesday
Strýc	Uncle, mother's brother. See Avunculus, Patruus
Stuprata L	Pregnant out of wedlock
S.U.P. L	Buried. See Pohřben, Humatus, Sepultus, Tumulatus
Svadba	Wedding. See Copulation, Solemmicatio
Švagr	Brother-in-law
Švagrova	Sister-in-law
Švatební oznámení	Wedding announcement. See Promulgation
Svátek	Holiday
Svátky	Usually means Christmas or Easter
Svobodník	A free farmer not obligated to work as a vassal. See Sedlák
Syn	See Puer
Synovec	Descendant. See Nepos, Patruelis

T

Tchán	Father-in-law
Tchýně	Mother-in-law
Tempus L	Time
Testament	Testament. See Kšaft, Poslední vůle
Teta	Aunt, mother's sister. See Anita, Matertera
Trigemini L	Triplets. See Trojčata
Trojčata	Triplets. See Trigemini

Tumulatus L	Buried. See Humatus, Pohřben, S.U.P., Sepultus
Tvrz	A well-protected residence occupied by the lesser nobility. See Hrad

U

Úmrtí	Death. See Mors, Mortia, Zesnutí
Unitas Fratrum	Religious society which originated from the followers of Jan Hus. See Bratrská Jednota
Únor	February
Urbář	See Gruntovní knihy. See chapter on "Sources for Genealogical Research in Czechoslovakia"
Úterý	Tuesday
Uxor L	Wife. See Manželka, Marita, Žena
Uxoratus L	Married

V

V cizoložství zplozené	Illegitimate child. See Děti
Vdova	Widow. See Relicta
Vdovec	Widower. See Vedovus
Vedovus	Widower. See Vdovec
Vejrunky	Liens against the farm. It could be moneys owed to the members of the immediate family by the one who inherited the property, or money owed for taxes.
Vir L	Man
Virgo L	Virgin. See Panna, Puella
Vlastní děti	Parents' own children. See Děti
Vnouče	Nephew, descendant. See Nepos
Vnučka	Granddaughter. See Neptis
Vnuk	Grandson
Vražda	Murder. See Homicidium

Výhost	Permission given to a vassal to move to another area. See Poddanství
Výměnkář(ka)	Retired farmer, living on his former property, supported by the son who inherited the farm. Suffix "ka" indicates female gender
Vyvážení	See Robota, Nevolnictví, Poddanství
Vývod	A listing of all ancestors of one individual

Z

záduší	Endowment; sum alloted to the church in a will
Zahradník	Owner of a cottage with a small plot for a garden. See Chalupník, Domkář, Sedlák
Zákonné děti	Of married parents. See Děti
Zalíbený, zalíbená	Adopted. Suffix "a" indicates female gender
Zámek	Pretentious residence of nobility. See Hrad
Zaměstnání	Occupation
Září	September
Zasnoubení	Engagement
Zeman	An ancient Czech word for svobodník, a free farmer not obligated to work as a vassal. See Sedlák
Zemřel(a)	Died. Suffix "a" indicates female gender
Zemské desky	Records of procedures under the highest court in Bohemia and Moravia. See Kvartery
Zemský soud	Federal court. See Soud
žena	Wife, woman. See Marita, Manželka, Uxor
ženich	Bridegroom

Zesnutí	Death. See Mors, Mortia, Úmrtí
Zeť	Male cousin. See Gener
Žid	Jew
Zima, v zimě	Winter, in winter
Živnost	Trade (suggests that the individual owned his own business)
Životní děti	When mother is one's own. See Děti
Značky rodopisné	Signs used in records other than matriky, indicating the type of event: * - birth + - death ∞ - marriage □ - man 0 - woman
Znak	Coat of arms. See Erb

SOME OF THE OCCUPATIONS MENTIONED IN MATRIKY AND OLD DOCUMENTS

Czech	Latin	German	English
Barvíř	Tinktor	Faerber	Dyer
Bečvár or bednář		Fassbinder	Maker of wooden pails
Bradýř, holič, ranhojič		Bartscherer	Barber, physic
Brašnár, see Tobolár		Taschner	Pursemaker
Brusič, see Slejfíř		Schleisser	Sharpener, honer
Caltar, pekař placek			Baker of pancakes
Chalupník	Sasarius	Haeusler	Cottager
Cikán	Cingarius	Zigeuner	Gypsy
Dělník, see Robotník	Operarius, opifex	Arbeiter	Laborer, vassal
Dohazovač, see Litkupník		Unterhaendler	Matchmaker
Domkár, see Chalupník			Cottager
Držitel, see Usedlík	Assesor	Besitzer	Settler
Duchovní	Clericus	Pfarrer	Priest
Farár	Clericus	Pfarrer	Minister (in charge of parish)

Czech	Latin	German	English
Flasnýr, see Klempíř		Klempner	Metalworker
Fojt, see Správce	Praefectus	Verwalter	Overseer
Fortnýr, see Vrátný		Torwaechter	Gatekeeper
Handlíř, see Kupec, Obchodník		Kaufman	Merchant; could be a peddler
Holič, see Bradýř			Barber
Hrstník, see Krupař		Graupner	
Jirchař		Weissgerger	Tanner
Kárník			Jail guard
Klempíř, see Flasnýr			Metalworker
Kolář	Carpentarius	Wagner	Wheelwright
Koloděj			Wheelwright
Kominík, see Mestkomín		Kaminfeger	Chimney sweep
Komoří	Cubicularius	Kaemmerer	Chamber attendant
Koňák, see Maštalíř		Pferdeknecht	Stable hand
Kostelník	Aedilus	Kirchendiener	Church clerk
Kovář	Faber	Schmied	Smith
Kramář, see Šmejdíř	Institor	Kraemer	Traveling merchant
Krejčí	Sartor	Schneider	Tailor
Krumplíř			Dealer in laces
Krupař, see Hrstník			
Kupec, see Handlíř			Merchant
Lázenský	Balneator		Keeper of the public bath
Lékař	Archister	Arzt	Physician
Lesník	Silvanus	Foerster	Forester
Litkupník, see Dohazovač			Matchmaker
Maštalir see Koňák			Stablehand
Medař, see Včelar		Bienenzuechter	Beekeeper
Měšťan, see Občan, Oby-vatel	Civis, Burgensis	Buerger	Citizen, burgher
Měšťanka, Mestkomín, see Kominik	Civissa	Buergerin	Female citizen
Městský písař	Secretarius	Schreiber	City scribe
Mlynář	Molitor, pistor	Mueller	Miller

Czech	Latin	German	English
Myslivec	Venator	Jaeger	Forester
Občan, see Měšťan			Citizen, burger
Obchodník, see Handlíř			Merchant
Obyvatel, see Měšťan		Bewohner	Citizen, burger
Oráč, see Rataj		Pflueger	Plower
Ozdobník			Dealer in laces
Pacholek	Famulus	Knecht	Farm servant
Pachtýř	Arendator		Tenant
Papírník	Chartarius	Papierhaendler	Paper merchant
Pecnář		Brotbaecker	Baker of bread
Pekař	Pistorius	Baeker	Baker
Písař	Scriptor	Schreiber	Scribe
Platnýř			Armormaker
Podruh	Inquilinius	Mietmann	Farm laborer
Posel	Tabellarius	Bote	Messenger
Pravovárečník			Citizen who has a right to make beer
Prťák		Schuhflicker	Shoe repairman
Puškar, see Ručníkař		Buechsemaker	Gunsmith
Ranhojič, see Bradýř			Barber
Rataj, see Oráč			Plow
Řemeslník	Merchanicus	Handworker	Tradesman
Řezník	Carnifex	Fleischbauer	Butcher
Robotník, see Dělník			Laborer, vassal
Rozárník			Maker of rosaries
Ručníkař, see Puškar			Gunsmith
Sanytrník			Maker of gunpowder
Sedlák	Rusticus	Bauer	Farmer
Slejfíř, see Brusič			Sharpener, honer
Smejdíř, see Kramář			Traveling merchant
Smukir			Peddler of notions
Správce, see Fojt			Overseer
Stavitel	Aedificator	Baumeister	Builder
Štejkyř			Mine overseer
Švec	Calciator, Sutor	Schuster	Shoemaker
Svícník, see Voskař			Candlemaker

Czech	Latin	German	English
Svíňák		Schweinhirt	Swineherd
Tarmarečník, see Vetešník		Troedler	Merchant with secondhand articles
Tesař	Faber, Lignarius	Zimmermann	Carpenter
Tkadlec	Textor	Weber	Weaver
Tobolář, see Brašnář			Pursemaker
Trhovník			Fair merchant
Truhlář	Arcularius	Tischler	Cabinetmaker
Uhlíř	Carbonarius	Koehler	Coalman
Usedlík, see Držitel			Settler
Vackař			Pursemaker
Vážník,			Scalemaker
Včelář, see Medař			Beekeeper
Vetešník, see Tarmarečník			Merchant with secondhand articles
Voják	Miles	Soldat	Soldier
Voskař, see Svíčník			Candlemaker
Vozka	Auriga	Kutcher	Coachman
Vratný, see Fortnýr			Gatekeeper
Zámečník	Claustrarius	Schlosser	Locksmith
Zbrojnoš	Armiger	Waffentraeger	Armed guard
Zemědelec	Agrocila		Agriculturist
Zlatník	Aurifaber	Goldarbeiter	Goldsmith

BIBLIOGRAPHY

Dixon, Charlton. SLOVAK GRAMMAR FOR ENGLISH SPEAKING STUDENTS. Pittsburgh, P.V. Rovnianek & Co., 1896.

Ertl, Václav. GEBAUEROVA MLUVNICE ČESKÁ. Prague: Československá grafická Unie, 1926. In Czech.

> Gebauer's Czech grammar book for secondary schools and teacher's institutes. Although old, this is the most scholarly work on the subject.

Havránek, Bohuslav, and Jedlička, Alois. STRUČNÁ MLUVNICE ČESKÁ. Prague: Státní pedagogické nakladatelstvi, 1956. In Czech.

> Abbreviated Czech grammar book.

Horecky, Pal I. CZECH AND SLOVAK ABBREVIATIONS. Washington, D.C.: Library of Congress, 1956. GL microfilm 812,987.

JAZYKOVEDNÝ ČASOPIS. Bratislava, 1950. In Czech.

Magazine of philology.

Jonas, Karel. BOHEMIAN MADE EASY; A PRACTICAL BOHEMIAN COURSE FOR ENGLISH SPEAKING PEOPLE. Racine, Wis., 1890. 2d ed. SLAVIE, 1900.

Kárník, Jan Jiří. MLUVNICE JAZYKA ČESKÉHO. New York, 1912. In Czech.

Czech grammar. Although old, its value for genealogists has not diminished. The newest rulings of grammar are not necessary for one who searches through old records.

Konus, Joseph James. PRACTICAL SLOVAK GRAMMAR WITH AN EXTENSIVE ENGLISH-SLOVAK AND SLOVAK-ENGLISH VOCABULARY. Pittsburgh: Author, 1939.

Lee, William Rowland, and Zdena, Lee. TEACH YOURSELF CZECH. New York: David Mackay Co., 1959.

Suitable for English-speaking people.

Mikula, Bohumil E. PROGRESSIVE CZECH. Chicago: Czechoslovak National Council of America, 1965.

Although slow in pace, it is popular in America and is used for teaching the Czech language in several colleges.

Šmejkalová, J., et al. SLOVAK-ENGLISH, SLOVAK POCKET DICTIONARY. Newark, N.J.: Vañous, 1972.

Sova, Miloš. A PRACTICAL CZECH COURSE. Vols. 1 and 2. Prague: Státní pedagogické nakladatelstvi, 1962. GL Ref 943.7 A8s.

For English-speaking students.

Trávníček, F. "Vlastní Substantiva." SBORNÍK PRACÍ FILOSOFICKÉ FAKULTY BRNĚNSKÉ UNIVERSITY. JAZYKOVĚDNÉ A Nos. 5-9 (1958). In Czech.

Concerns the grammar of names, based on nouns. Published by the University in Brno.

Collection of the samples of old and new handwritings of various nations, in possession of the Evaluation Department of the Genealogical Society in Salt Lake City. Not available to the public.

Chapter 10
NOBILITY AND HERALDRY

In the modern sense of the word, heraldry is a branch of history. Heraldic experts, however, consider their work to be an independent field of study. Though heraldry came into prominence quite late, several European universities offer courses on heraldic studies; and there are numerous periodicals from many countries which specialize in its study.

Heraldry is the study of coats of arms. These originated from the jousting tournaments of the Middle Ages where the nobility competed to prove their valor and skills. The court officials who kept the records of the participants and studied their coats of arms for authenticity and family connections were called heralds. With the passage of time, the heralds developed great knowledge concerning the coats of arms and were given additional responsibilities not directly related to the tournaments. They were assigned by the kings to paint the coats of arms on parchment, with every detail carefully noted or added as new slogans or meaningful embellishments were granted to the families. These parchment records are called armorials (in Czech, erbovníci) and represent an invaluable source of heraldic studies.

The nobility were the first to assume surnames. This practice was initiated in order to identify the individuals, both in written documents and at the Czech and other European courts. These first surnames were based on the name of the estate the family owned. "Z Dubé," for example, indicated a family from Dubá. However, often in the thirteenth and fourteenth centuries, as the people began shopping around for a more convenient place to live, properties were sold and bought; and the surnames had to be changed accordingly. Jan z Dubé might become Jan z Říčan. His surname may have been changed several times during the course of his lifetime. The study of coats of arms is very useful for tracing the alterations in a family surname. Fortunately, in the fifteenth century the nobility accepted more permanent surnames to which the name of the family residence was added: Jan Kozlovský z Dubé ("z" is an equivalent of French "de," German "von," or English "of" or "from."

Nobility and Heraldry

Titles of nobility were awarded by the kings, based on the recipient's military accomplishments or civil service. All advancements within the nobility were also bestowed by the king. The primary advantage of ennobled families was in the land ownership, which became a most important consideration in ruling the feudal society. In the twelfth century, the Czech nobility was divided into higher ranks (Vyšší panstvo: korouhevní--standard bearing, called Pán) and lesser ranks (vladykové, zemani, and rytíři). There also was a marked difference between the original nobility (původní) and new nobility (novoštítná). The titles of count (hrabě), baron, and Freiher (Svobodný Pán) were introduced much later, under the Austrian domination.

Certain historical events in Czechoslovakia gave rise to a special class of farmers whose large holdings and influence among the rest of the community's population gave them a special, privileged status. They were tolerated by the local landlords but were never officially ennobled. The times elevated them to a status of seminobility, but, after some few generations, these families disappeared in oblivion. Although many of them enjoyed high respect among their neighbors, they were counted as "new ones" and were not socially accepted by the old nobility. Statistics show that in Bohemia alone in 1615 there were 1,174 noble families (one fifth of them belonged to the "new ones"); in 1656, 500 families; in 1757, 276 families; and in 1843, 187 noble families.

The confusion concerning the nobility was also created by the procedure of the Hapsburgs, who, after the Thirty Years' War, rewarded participants--soldiers, military entrepreneurs, and bureaucrats--by giving them titles. These titles were, in fact, meaningless, since no property went with them. In addition, many foreign families moved to Bohemia in the second half of the eighteenth and the first half of the nineteenth centuries. The matriky and other documents would identify such individuals (or families) by flowery titles; but only searches of local archives or the nobiliary documents deposited in the Archives of the Ministry of Interior would prove their right to a true title of nobility.

The records of ennoblements prior to 1620 were registered at the royal court in Prague and are currently deposited in the Archives of the Ministry of Interior in Prague. Records of titles of nobility bestowed by the Austrian rulers to Czech individuals after 1620 were registered at the emperor's court in Vienna and were kept in the Department of Nobility of the Ministry of Interior in Vienna. After 1918 they were transferred to the Archives of the Ministry of Interior in Prague. There are 150 boxes of such records, including the official correspondence, all arranged in alphabetical order according to family surname. The Archives of the Ministry of Interior is not prepared to conduct searches of the material; all inquiries should be directed to the Czechoslovakian Embassy, 3900 Linnean Ave., N.W., Washington D.C. 20008.

After the disintegration of the Austro-Hungarian Empire and the creation of the Czechoslovak Republic in 1918, the use of all titles of nobility as well as the wearing of Austro-Hungarian orders or medals were abolished. The coats of arms were neither granted nor recognized after 1918. It was soon felt, however, that foreign political and military leaders should be awarded some token of recognition for their services, especially when they visited Czechoslovakia. Accordingly, in 1922, a bill was passed establishing the Czechoslovak Order of the White Lion (after the heraldic lion of Bohemia). This is not to be confused with the coats of arms pertaining to former nobility.

In the bibliography following this chapter, several Czech periodicals are listed that deal with the study of heraldry. Anyone interested in a more extensive study of heraldry should consult them. One of the foremost authorities on Czechoslovak heraldry is Adolf Karlovský (Wartenbergstr. 43, CHO 4127 Biersfelden, Basel, Switzerland). He is a member of the International College of Arms and can answer queries concerning Czech noble families.

Another renowned authority on coats of arms is Jiří Louda, presently an official in the State Science Library in Olomouc, Moravia, and a frequent contributor to the ARMORIAL AND INTERNATIONAL QUARTERLY JOURNAL. He has an extensive library of material concerning Czech heraldry and much valuable information pertaining to British nobility and nobility of other European nations.

Many genealogical researchers waste much effort and money when they endeavor to establish a connection between their ancestry and past nobility. To be sure, there is a certain glamour in being connected with a noble family, and there is a much better chance of finding more complete records than would exist for commoners. However, the only correct, reliable and efficient system of genealogical research is to proceed from the known to the unknown. This means it is necessary to verify each item of information on hand and only then proceed to search sources concerning the preceeding generation. If there is any connection between your family and nobility, it will come to light in the sources searched.

Genealogies of common families have been collected and printed in Czechoslovakia, although not in such large numbers as in other countries. Unfortunately, a summary bibliography of these volumes has never been issued. It is difficult to locate printed family histories of the Czech ancestors that pertain to Czech-Americans. If

Nobility and Heraldry

Czech-Americans are able to identify the author, title, publisher, place and date of publication of a family history published in Czechoslovakia, and they wish to purchase it, they should contact a book dealer that specializes in the exportation and sale of foreign books. One such dealer is ARTIA (Ve Smečkách 3, Prague). Some printed family genealogies have been purchased by the Genealogical Library. Reference to them can be found in the microfilm card catalog in any branch library. (See the chapter "The Genealogical Library of the Church of Jesus Christ of Latter-Day Saints."

GLOSSARY

Agnatus (L)	Male line of ancestors. See po meči.
Armiger	Shield bearer, candidate for knighthood. See panoš.
Baro	A title introduced in Bohemia under Austrian rule. See baron, svobodník.
Baron(ka)	Suffix "ka" indicates female gender. See baro.
Císař (cisařovna)	Emperor. See imperatus.
Císařstoi	Empire. See imperium.
Cognatvo (L)	Female line of ancestors. See po přeslici.
Comes (L)	Count. See hrabě.
Comitissa (L)	Countess. See hraběnka.
Conditus (L)	Honorable.
Dominis (L)	Sir. See pán.
Dux (L)	Duke. See vévoda.
Dynastes (L)	Nobleman. See šlechtic.
Erb	Coat of arms. See znak.
Erbnovík	Royal keeper of the coats of arms.
Generusus (L)	On noble birth. See urozený.
Heraldika	Heraldry.
Honestus (L)	Highly respectable (title). Form of addressing or referring to a nobleman.
Hrabě	Count. See comes.
Hraběnka	Countess. See comitissa.
Hrad	Residence of nobility in the Middle Ages.
Illustrus (L)	Illustrious.
Imperatrix (L)	Empress. See císař, (císařovna)
Imperatus (L)	Emperor. See císař.
Imperium (L)	See císařstvi.
Ingenuus (L)	Freeman. See svobodník.
Kmet	Lower nobility of the Middle Ages.
Kvartery	Records of the procedures in the highest court in Bohemia and Moravia. See zemské desky.
Leník	Vassal, recipient of léno. See léno.
Léno	Land and/or privileges given by the king or the local nobility to a leník (vassal) under certain conditions and an oath of loyalty. See leník, man.

Levoboček	Illegitimate child of a member of the noble class. Literal translation, "from the left hip."
List erbovní	Document granting the coat of arms.
Majestát	Grant of freedom, privilege or land, usually bestowed by the king.
Man	Vassal, recipient of léno. See léno.
Miles (L)	Knight. Member of the lower nobility. His principal purpose was to wage wars, usually on horseback. He was also to be a model Christian. See rytíř.
Nobilits (L)	Noble.
Nobilitace	Awarding the title of nobility.
Novoštítná šlechta	New nobility.
Pan	Lesser nobility. See dominis.
Panos	Shield bearer, candidate for knighthood. See armiger.
Patrimoniální správa	Summary of the political and tax rights of the feudal lords over the vassal, used only to 1848.
Pečet.	Seal. See sigillum.
Persona nobilis (L)	Honorable person.
Po meči	Male line of ancestors. See agnatus.
Po přeslici	Female line of ancestors. See cognatio.
Původní šlechta	Original nobility.
Regia Majestat	Royal majesty.
Regina (L)	Queen.
Regius (L)	Royal.
Rex (L)	King.
Rytíř	Member of the lower nobility. See miles.
Sigillum (L)	Seal. See pecet.
Sigillum Pendens (L)	Seal affixed to the document by a string.
Šlechta	Nobility.
Šlechtic	Nobleman. See dynastes.
Svobodník	Freeman. See ingenuus.
Tvrz	Fortress.
Urozený	On noble birth. See generusus.
Vévoda	See dux.
Vyšší Panstvo	Higher nobility.
Vysoce Vážený	See honestus.
Zámek	Pretentious homes of the nobility, built in the seventeenth century and after.
Zeman	Lower nobility.
Zemské Desky	Records of the procedures in the highest court on Bohemia and Moravia. See kvartery.
Znak	Coat of arms. See erb.

BIBLIOGRAPHY

ANCESTRY OF FREDERICK PHILIPSE, FIRST LORD AND FOUNDER OF PHILIPSE MANOR AT YONKERS. New York: The Peabar Co.,1939.

AUGUSTINE HERMAN OF BOHEMIA MANOR. Prague: State Printing Office, 1939.

Bačkovský, Rudolf. BÝVALÁ ČESKÁ ŠLECHTA PŘEDBĚLOHORSKÁ A POBĚLOHORSKÁ NA SVÝCH SÍDLECH V ČECHACH A NA MORAVĚ A VE SVÝCH ZNACÍCH. Prague: Jindřich Bačkovský, 1948. GL 943.7 D22b. In Czech.

Former Czech nobility before 1620 and after 1620, their estates and coats of arms.

Bek, A. RODOKMEN V PRAKSI. Prague, Školní naklad, 1941. In Czech.

Genealogy in usage.

Capek, Karel. HOVORY S T.G. MASARYKEM. Prague: František Borový, 1935. In Czech.

The same work as that cited below.

_____. PRESIDENT MASARYK TELLS HIS STORY. London: George Allen, 1934.

Discussions with President Masaryk (1918-37).

ČASOPIS RODOPISNÉ SPOLEČNOSTI ČESKOSLOVENSKÉ V PRAZE. Prague, 1929-44. GL 943.6 B2c. In Czech.

The most extensive genealogical periodical published in Czechoslovakia, now discontinued.

ČASOPIS SPOLEČNOSTI PŘÁTEL STAROŽITNOSTÍ. Prague, 1893. In Czech.

Journal of the history and geography of Bohemia. Notes on documents; book reviews. Includes author and topographical index. No longer in existence.

ČASOPIS VLASTENECKÉHO SPOLKU MUSEJNÍHO V OLOMOUCI. Olomouc, Moravia: Patriotic Museum Society, 1925. GL 943.72 B2v (only 1936). In Czech.

Czechoslovakian Families

Beneš, František, ed. DĚJINY--ROD--TRADICE. Prague: Svaz přátel rodopisu (Society of Friends of Genealogy), 1940.

Chaloupecky, Václav. KNÍŽE SVATÝ VÁCLAV. Prague: Historický klub, 1947. GL 921.437 Al no. 3. In Czech.

Biography of Saint Wenceslas, Duke of Bohemia, 910-29.

Chalupný, Emanuel. ŽIŽKA. Prague: Melantrich, 1924. GL 921.437 Al no. 5. In Czech.

Biography of General Žižka of Trocnov, an important figure in the Hussite Wars.

Davídek, V. STARÉ USEDLÉ RODY SEISKÉ V ČECHÁCH. Posloup-
nost Hospodárů ve 128 Usedlostech. Prague, 1941. Reprinted
in Rodopisná Galerie VI, supplement of the ČASOPIS RODO-
PISNÉ SPOLEČNOSTI 13 (1941). In Czech.

> Ancient farm families in Bohemia. The succession of
> the owners of 128 settlements.

Doerr, August. ADEL DER BOEMISCHEN KRONLAENDER. 8 vols.
Prague: Franz Rivnac, 1900. In German.

> The nobility of the Bohemian crown lands; proofs of
> their coats of arms and diplomas of nobility as
> registered at the Ministery of Interior, Vienna.

Dvorský, František. O STAROŽITNÉM PANSKÉM RODĚ BENEŠOVICŮ.
Brno: Musejní spolek, 1907. In Czech.

> About the ancient noble family of Benesovice from
> Moravia.

ERB RYTIŘSKÉ RODINY TRMALŮ Z TOUŠIC. Kupfer, n.d. GL 943.7
A22c. In Czech.

> The coat of arms of the family of knights Trmal from
> Toušice by Poděhrady, Bohemia.

HERALDICKÝ ČASOPIS. Prague: Heraldická Společnost, 1968.
In Czech.

Heymann, Frederick Gotthold. GEORGE OF BOHEMIA, KING OF
HERETICS. Princeton, N.J.: Princeton University Press,
1965. GL 921.437 J566h.

"Hlasatel." Collector nos. 1, 2, and 4. Prague: Klub
sběratelů kuriosit, n.d. GL 943.7 D24h. In Czech.

> Heraldic genealogical supplement of this monthly
> publication.

Holeček, Josef. ČESKÁ ŠLECHTA. Co Vám Chci Říci Series.
Prague, 1918. GL 943.7 D22h. In Czech.

> Czech nobility.

Horníček, Ignac. KNIHA O RODOPISU. Vyškov, Czechoslovakia:
1939. In Czech.

> About genealogy. Practical introduction to genealogy,
> with a supplement concerning community chronicles.

Hosák, L. MORAVSKO-SLEZSKÉ PRAMENY K SELSKÉMU RODOPISU.
Kronikářský list no. 13. Prague: Sdruženi venkovských
kronikařů, 1923. In Czech.

> Moravian-Silesian sources for rural genealogies.

Houdek, V. MORAVSKÉ VÝVODY ERBOVNÍ. Brno: Musejní spolek, 1917. GL P.B.A. 1599. In Czech.

Moravian coats of arms.

Hrubý, František. LADISLAV VELÉN ZE ŽEROTÍNA. Prague: Historicky klub, 1930. GL 931.437 Z54h. In Czech.

Biography of Ladislav Velén of Žerotín, 1579-1638.

Jelínek, Břetislav. DIE BOEHMEN IM KAMPFE UM IHRE SELBS-STAENDIGKEIT, 1618-1648. Prague: Taussig & Taussig, 1916. GL microfilm 24390. In Czech.

This describes the Czechs in their battle for self-determination during the years 1618-48. Contains genealogies and biographies of the Czech warriors in the Thirty Years' War.

Kalista, Zdeněk. ZIKMUND MYSLÍK Z HYRŠOVA. Prague: Českomoravský kompas, 1940. GL 921.437 Al No. 4. In Czech.

Biography of Zikmund Myslík of Hyršov, noble of Bohemia. Died 1666.

KAREL IV. Prague: Melantrich, 1946. GL 921.437 K145k. In Czech.

Biography of Charles IV, king of Bohemia.

Karlovský, Adolf F. ZAKLADY HERALDIKY. Prague. Československenská společnost přátel drobné plastiky, 1966. In Czech.

Basics of heraldry.

Král, Adalbert. RITTER VON DOBRÁ VODA. Prague: Taussig, 1904. In German.

Discusses the knights of Dobrá Voda. Genealogical and heraldic analysis, with sources and coats of arms.

Krejčík, Ad. L. Z BIBLIOGRAFIE LITERÁRNÍCH POMŮCEK RODO-PISCOVÝCH. Reprint. Prague: Časopis Rodopisné společnosti, V, 1939. In Czech.

Bibliography of literary aids to genealogists.

Markus-Ratkovich. PŘÍRUCKA RODINNÉHO KRONIKÁŘE. ÚVOD DO PRAKTICKÉ GENEALOGIE. 2d, rev. ed. Prague: Knihovna Rodopisné společnosti, no. 7, 1938. In Czech.

Very good handbook for a family chronicler. An introduction to practical genealogy.

Maršán, B. JIŘÍ Z PODĚBRAD TVŮRCE SPOŘÁDANÉHO STÁTU, 1420-1471. Jičín, Bohemia: Musejní spolek, 1937. GL 921. 437 Al, no. 1. In Czech.

Biography of Jiří of Poděbrady, elected Czech king, creator of a well-organized state, 1420-71.

Mejtský, Josef. PŘÍSPĚVKY K DĚJINÁM ŠLECHTY V ČECHÁCH, S PŘIPOJENÍM RODOPISU NEBESKÝCH Z VOJKOVIC. Prague: N.p., 1901. GL 932.71 D22m. In Czech.

Contribution to the history of the nobility in Bohemia: an ancestry of knights of Nebeský of Vojkovice has been added.

Merhout, Cyril. DĚTI ČESKÝCH KRÁLŮ. Prague: Společnost přátel starožitností, 1938. GL 943.7 D22m. In Czech.

The children of Czech kings.

Moeschler, Felix. ALTE HERRNHUTER FAMILIES. Herrnhut, Missionbuchhandlung, 1922. GL 932.212 D2n. In German.

The old Herrnhut families. Published on the occasion of the two-hundredth anniversary of the Herrnhut Brotherhood.

Novotný, Václav. ČESKÝ KNÍŽE VÁCLAV SVATÝ. Prague: Státní nakladatelství, 1929. GL 921.437 Al no. 2. In Czech.

Biography of Saint Wenceslaus, Duke of Bohemia, 910-29.

Odlozilik, Otakar. THE HUSSITE KING: BOHEMIA IN EUROPEAN AFFAIRS, 1440-1471. New Brunswick, N.J.: Rutgers University Press, 1965. GL 943.7 H2o.

King Jiří Poděbrady was called the Hussite King.

_____. KAREL STARŠÍ ZE ŽEROTÍNA, 1564-1636. Prague: Melantrich, 1936. GL 921.437 Z540. In Czech.

Life of Karel of Žerotín, Moravian nobleman, 1564-1636.

Palacký, František. DĚJINY NÁRODU ČESKÉHO V ČECHÁCH A NA MORAVĚ. Prague· B. Kočí, 1907. GL microfilm 446,642. In Czech.

The most scholarly work on Bohemian and Moravian history. Includes numerous genealogies of nobility.

Palivec, Viktor. RODINA A RODOKMEN. Prague: N.p., 1939. In Czech.

Concise instructions for genealogical work.

Pekař, Josef. SVATÝ VÁCLAV. Reprint. Prague: Historický klub, 1932. GL 921.437 V137p. In Czech.

Special reprint of the collections concerning Saint Wenceslaus, duke of Bohemia, 910-29.

Pokorný, František. ŠVABENICE, ROD PÁNŮ ZE ŠVABENIC. Brno: Musejní spolek, 1970. GL 943.723/S 1 H2p. In Czech.

History of the town of Švabenice, Moravia and its estate owners. Contains genealogical tables, maps.

Prochazka, Roman Freiherr von. GENEALOGISCHES HANDBUCH ERSCHLOSENER BOEMISCHER HERRENSTANDTSFAMILIEN. Neustadt/ Aisch: Degener & Co., 1973. GL 943.7 D22p. In German.

Genealogical handbook of the extinct Bohemian nobility.

Radostický, J.P. KRALOVÉHRADECKÉ, CHRUDIMSKÉ, PRAŽSKÉ, A.J. RODINY ERBOVNÍ A MĚSTANSKÉ. Vienna: N.p., 1909. In Czech.

The heraldic and estate families from Hradec Kralove, Chrudim, and Prague districts. Heraldic and genealogical contributions.

Rybícka, A. KRALOVÉHRADECKÉ RODINY ERBOVNÍ. Special reprint from REVIEWS OF THE ROYAL BOHEMIAN SOCIETY OF SCIENCES. Prague: Královská česká společnost nauk, 1873.

Heraldic families from Hradec Kralové.

SBORNIK JEDNOTY POTOMKŮ POBĚLOHORSKÝCH EXULANTŮ-POKUTNIKE A PRATEL RODOPISU V. PRAZE. Prague, 1930. Eight issues only.

Magazine of the Union of the Descendants of the Exultants After the Battle on the White Mountain (1620) and of the Friends of Genealogy.

SBORNÍK JEDNOTY STARÝCH ČESKÝCH RODŮ. RODOPIS. DĚJINY, HERALDIKA. 1930-1937. Prague.

Genealogy, History, Heraldry. Journal of the Association of Old Czech Families.

Sedláček, August. "O Staročeských Příjmeních Šlechtických." SBORNÍK FILOLOGICKY 7 (1922): 41-62. In Czech.

Concerning old Czech surnames of the nobility.

_____. ZÁMKY A TVRZE KRÁLOVSTVÍ ČESKÉHO. Prague: n.p., 1882-1936. GL G 943.7 22s. In Czech.

Fortresses, castles and manors in Bohemia and Moravia. Contains numerous pedigrees of nobility and extracts from old documents and wills. Indispensable for genealogical research.

Urbánek, Rudolf. KONEC LADISLAVA POHROBKA. [The end of Ladislav Pohrobek] Prague: Česká akademie věd a umění, 1924. GL 921.437 Ll25u. In Czech.

King of Bohemia, 1440-1457.

_____. O VOLBĚ JIŘÍHO Z PODĚBRAD ZA KRÁLE ČESKÉHO. Prague: Československá akademie věd a umění, 1924. GL 943.7 H2u. In Czech.

Study of the election of Jiří of Poděbrady as king of Bohemia on March 2, 1458.

Von Wurzbach, Constant. BIOGRAPHISCHES LEXIKON DES KAISER-THUMS OESTERREICH. 60 vols. Vienna: Verlag der Universitaeta-Buchdruckerei, 1856. GL Ref 920.0436 W966b or microfilm 599,385. In German.

Biographic dictionary of the Austrian empire. Includes life sketches of prominent people that lived in the empire from 1750-1850. Many Bohemians, Moravians and Slovaks are included.

Vysín, Karel, ed. HERALDIKA, BULLETIN PRO ZÁKLADNÍ VĚDY HISTORICKÉ. Prague, 1967. In Czech. Editor's address: 252-06, Davle 174, Prague-Západ, Czechoslovakia.

Wurmova, Milada. SOUPIS MORAVSKÝCH NOVIN A ČASOPISŮ Z LET 1848-1918. Brno: Krajské nakladetelství, 1955. GL 943.7 A1, no. 3. In Czech.

Bibliography of the newspapers and periodicals in Moravia, 1848-1918.

Chapter 11

CONCLUSION

Until the first part of the last century, genealogical research was conducted primarily for practical and legal purposes, or else either to gain or maintain family privileges and properties. However, since the latter nineteenth century, genealogy has developed into one of the auxiliary branches of history, exerting a marked impact on other studies as well. The legal implications of research are enhanced by information concerning the biological evolution of the family. Demography and sociology have gained invaluable assistance from genealogical studies. Genealogical research has yielded important data relating to the cultural and intellectual development of entire communities.

None of this would have much value if genealogical research were limited only to families of the nobility or privileged classes. Information concerning all social groups is necessary, especially when we consider that in the past the great majority of people were not privileged or otherwise distinguished. The last one hundred fifty years mark an unprecedented interest in genealogical research, which, according to the latest estimates, has become the second largest "hobby" of all the social classes in this country. This healthy curiosity and pride in our ancestry is commendable, especially in our country where the only indigenous people are the native American Indians. The ancestors of all other citizens came from other parts of the world. For those who want to know about their Czech and Slovak forefathers, it is my hope that the information contained here will help Czech-Americans successfully trace their ancestral lines.

Since many beginners in genealogical research do not know how to start, following are some basic suggestions:

1. Make a recording of your own immediate family, collecting all vital dates, places and full names, leaving out no member of the family,(even if the person died as an infant). For the most complete results use the printed family group forms, which can be obtained from the closest Latter-Day Saint Branch Library (see their list at the end of the book), or in quantity from Everton Publishers, Logan, Utah.

2. Complete a similar record for the preceding generation, for both the father's and mother's lineage. Each individual should be completely identified by listing his full name, date and place of birth, marriage and death. Incomplete dates and "supposed" places are not acceptable.

3. Proceed thus from known to unknown, using suggestions included in the chapter "Czech and Slovak Immigration to America."

4. Read the chapter on "Sources for Genealogical Research in Czechoslovakia." Evaluate your research objective and determine which sources to use. Locate the sources, request their search, and from the reports obtained, record the findings.

All this work requires much time, care, and expense. The results should be neatly sorted. Other families of the same line might be interested in obtaining a copy of your genealogical manuscript. The local public library or historical society may also desire a copy for their files.

GENEALOGICAL RESEARCH FOR CZECH AND SLOVAK AMERICANS has been compiled, written and published for you to study and use in your genealogical research. I hope it will serve you well. My sincere wishes for your success.

Appendix 1
BRANCH GENEALOGICAL LIBRARIES OF THE CHURCH
OF JESUS CHRIST OF LATTER-DAY SAINTS

ALABAMA

Huntsville Alabama Stake
Branch Genealogy Library
106 Sanders Drive, S.W.
Huntsville, Alabama 35803

ALASKA

Anchorage Alaska Stake
Branch Genealogy Library
2591 Maplewood Street
Anchorage, Alaska 99509

Fairbanks Alaska District
Branch Genealogy Library
1500 Cowles Street
Fairbanks, Alaska 99701

ARIZONA

Flagstaff Arizona Stake
Branch Genealogy Library
625 East Cherry
Flagstaff, Arizona 86001
          PROPOSED

Globe Arizona Stake
428 Sutherland
Globe, Arizona 85532
          PROPOSED

Holbrook Arizona Stake
Branch Genealogy Library
1600 N. 2d Avenue
Holbrook, Arizona 86025

Mesa Arizona Branch
Genealogy Library
464 East First Avenue
Mesa, Arizona 85204

St. David Arizona Stake
Branch Genealogy Library
St. David Stake Center
St. David, Arizona 85630

Safford Arizona Branch
Genealogy Library
808 8th Avenue
Safford, Arizona 85546

Phoenix Arizona North
Branch Genealogy Library
8602 N. 31st Avenue
Phoenix, Arizona 85019

Phoenix Arizona West
Stake Genealogy Library
3102 N. 18th Avenue
Phoenix, Arizona 85033

Prescott Arizona Stake
Branch Genealogy Library
1001 Ruth Street
Prescott, Arizona 86301

St. Johns Arizona Stake
Branch Genealogy Library
Stake Center
35 West Cleveland Street
St. Johns, Arizona 85936

Show Low Arizona Stake
Branch Genealogy Library
          PROPOSED

Snowflake Arizona Branch
Genealogy Library
Hunt Avenue
Snowflake, Arizona 85937

Tucson Arizona Branch
Genealogy Library
Stake Center
500 South Langley
Tucson, Arizona 85710

Yuma Arizona Stake
Branch Genealogy Library
6th Avenue & 17th Street
Yuma, Arizona 85634

ARKANSAS

Little Rock Arkansas
Stake Branch Genealogy
Library
PROPOSED

AUSTRALIA

Adelaide Australia Stake
Branch Genealogy Library
120 Gage Street
Firle, South Australia 5070

Melbourne Australia
Branch Genealogy Library
285 Heidelberg Road
Northcote, Victoria
Australia 3084

Australian Microfilm
Ordering Center
Percival W.F. Davis,
Director
P.O. Box 218
Greensboro, 3088
Victoria, Australia

Parramatta Australia Stake
Branch Genealogy Library
100 Westbank Avenue
Emu Plains, NSW 2750
Australia
PROPOSED

Perth Australia Stake
Branch Genealogy Library
163 Wordsworth Avenue
Yokine, Western Australia
6060
PROPOSED

Sydney Australia
Branch Genealogy Library
55 Greenwich Road
Greenwich, Sydney
Australia 2065

Sydney Australia South
Stake Branch Genealogy
Library
Sutherland Ward Chapel
196 Bath Road
Kirrawee, NSW, Australia
2232

CALIFORNIA

Anaheim California Branch
Genealogy Library
440 North Loara (Rear)
Anaheim, California 92803

Bakersfield California
Stake Branch Genealogy
Library
1903 Bernard Street
Bakersfield, California
93306

Barstow California Stake
Branch Genealogy Library
2571 Barstow Road
Barstow, California 92311

Cerritos California Stake
Branch Genealogy Library
17909 Bloomfield
Cerritos, California 90701
PROPOSED

Cerritos California West
Stake Branch Genealogy
Library
15311 S. Pioneer Boulevard
Norwalk, California 90650
PROPOSED

Chico California Stake
Branch Genealogy Library
Stake Center
1528 Esplanade
Chico, California 95926

Covina California Stake
Branch Genealogy Library
656 S. Grand Avenue
Covina, California 91790

Escondido California
Stake Genealogy Library
Stake Center
1917 E. Washington
Escondido, California
92025
             PROPOSED

Eureka California Stake
Branch Genealogy Library
2734 Dolbeer
Eureka, California 95501

Fresno California Branch
Genealogy Library
1838 Echo
Fresno, California 93738

Gridley California Stake
Branch Genealogy Library
348 Spruce Street
Gridley, California 95948

La Crescenta California
Stake Branch Genealogy
Library
             PROPOSED

Long Beach California East
Stake Branch Genealogy
Library
Stake Center
1140 Ximeno
Long Beach, California 90804

Los Angeles California
Branch Genealogy Library
10741 Santa Monica Boulevard
Los Angeles, California
90025

Los Angeles California East
Branch Genealogy Library
106 South Hillview Avenue
Los Angeles, California
91803

Modesto California Branch
Genealogy Library
LDS Chapel
731 El Vista Avenue
Modesto, California 95380

Monterey California Stake
Branch Genealogy Library
Corner Noche Buena 7 Plumas
Seaside, California 93955

Oakland California Branch
Genealogy Library
4780   Lincoln Avenue
Oakland, California 94602

Redding California Stake
Branch Genealogy Library
3410 Churn Creek Road
Redding, California 96001

Riverside California
Branch Genealogy Library
5900 Grand Avenue
Riverside, California 92504

Riverside California West
Stake Branch Genealogy
Library
4375 Jackson Street
Riverside, California
92503

Ridgecrest California
Stake Branch Genealogy
Library
501 Norma Street
Ridgecrest, California
93527

Sacramento California
Branch Genealogy Library
2745 Eastern Avenue
Sacramento, California
95825

San Bernardino California
Stake Branch Genealogy
Library
Stake Center
7000 Central Avenue
San Bernardino, California
92403

San Diego California
Branch Genealogy Library
3705 10th Avenue
San Diego, California 92103

San Jose California
Branch Genealogy Library
1336 Cherry Avenue
San Jose, California 95150

San Luis Obispo California
Stake Branch Genealogy
Library
55 Casa Street
San Luis Obispo, California
93401

Santa Barbara California
Branch Genealogy Library
478 Cambridge Drive
Goleta, California 93107

Santa Clara California
Branch Genealogy Library
875 Quince Avenue
Santa Clara, California
95051

Santa Maria California
Stake Branch Genealogy
Library
1312 W. Prune Avenue
Lompoc, California 93436

Santa Rosa California
Stake Branch Genealogy
Library
1725 Peterson Lane
Santa Rosa, California
95401

Simi Valley California
Stake Branch Genealogy
Library
5028 E. Cochran
Simi Valley, California
93063
                    PROPOSED

Stockton California Stake
Branch Genealogy Library
San Joaquin Stake Center
814 Brookside Road
Stockton, California 95206

Upland California Stake
Branch Genealogy Library
Stake Center
785 N. San Antonio
Upland, California 91786
                    PROPOSED

Ventura California Branch
Genealogy Library
3501 Loma Vista Road
Ventura, California 93003

Whittier California Stake
Branch Genealogy Library
7906 S. Pickering
Whittier, California 90604

CANADA

Calgary Alberta Branch
Genealogy Library
2021 17th Avenue S.W.
Calgary, Alberta, Canada
121-0G2

Cardston Alberta Branch
Genealogy Library
348 Third Street West
Cardston, Alberta, Canada
T0K OKO

Edmonton Alberta Stake
Branch Genealogy Library
9010 85th Street
Edmonton, Alberta, Canada
T6H 3J2

Lethbridge Alberta
Branch Genealogy Library
Stake Center
2410 28th Street S.
Lethbridge, Alberta,
Canada T1J 3R7

Ottawa Ontario Dist.
Branch Genealogy Library
1017 Prince of Wales Drive
Ottawa, Ontario, Canada
                    PROPOSED

Toronto Ontario
Branch Genealogy Library
95 Melbert Street
Etobicoke, Ontario,
Canada

Vancouver B.C. Stake
Branch Genealogy Library
Stake Center
5280 Kincaid
Burnaby 2, Vancouver, B.C.
Canada V53 358

Vernon British Columbia
Stake Genealogy Library
           PROPOSED

COLORADO

Arvada Colorado Stake
Branch Genealogy
           PROPOSED

Boulder Colorado Stake
Branch Genealogy Library
4655 Table Mesa Drive
Boulder, Colorado 80203

Colorado Springs Colorado
Stake Branch Genealogy
Library
Stake Center
Colorado Springs, Colorado
80906

Denver Colorado Branch
Genealogy Library
Denver Stake Center
740 Hudson Street
Denver, Colorado 80220

Denver Colorado North Stake
Branch Genealogy Library
100 E. Malley Drive
Northglenn, Colorado 80233

Durango Colorado Stake
Branch Genealogy Library
1800 E. Empire Street
Cortez, Colorado 81321

Fort Collins Colorado Stake
Branch Genealogy Library
Ft. Collins Ward
1400 Lynnwood Drive
Ft. Collins, Colorado 80521

Grand Junction Colorado
Stake
Branch Genealogy Library
Grand Junction Stake Center
543 Melody Lane
Grand Junction, Colorado
81501

LaJara Colorado Stake
Branch Genealogy Library
Stake Center
LaJara, Colorado 81140

Littleton Colorado Stake
Branch Genealogy Library
1939 E. Easter Avenue
Littleton, Colorado 80121
           PROPOSED

CONNECTICUT

Hartford Connecticut Stake
Branch Genealogy Library
30 Woodside Avenue
Manchester, Connecticut
06080

ENGLAND

Huddersfield England Stake
Branch Genealogy Library
Stake Center
Halifax Road
Birchencliffe, Huddersfield,
England
           PROPOSED

Nottingham England
Branch Genealogy Library
Loughborough Ward Chapel
Alan Moss Road
Loughborough, Leicester,
England
           PROPOSED

Sunderland England Stake
Branch Genealogy Library
Stake Center
Alexandra Road
Sunderland, Tyne & Wear,
England
PROPOSED

FLORIDA

Jacksonville Florida
Branch Genealogy Library
4087 Hendricks Avenue
Jacksonville, Florida
32211

Miami Florida Branch
Genealogy Library
1350 N.W. 95th Street
Miami, Florida 33147

Orlando Florida Stake
Branch Genealogy Library
45 E. Par Avenue
Orlando, Florida 32804

Pensacola Florida Stake
Branch Genealogy Library
5673 North 9th Avenue
Pensacola, Florida 32522

Tallahassee Florida Stake
Branch Genealogy Library
Stake Center
312 Stadium Drive
Tallahassee, Florida 32303

Tampa Florida Stake
Branch Genealogy Library
4106 Fletcher Avenue
Tampa, Florida 33612

GEORGIA

Macon Georgia Stake
Branch Genealogy Library
3006 14th Avenue
Columbus, Georgia 31905

Sandy Springs Georgia Stake
Branch Genealogy Library
1155 Mt. Vernon Highway
Dunwoody, Georgia 30338

HAWAII

Kaneohe Hawaii Stake
Branch Genealogy Library
46-117 Halaulani Street
Kaneohe, Hawaii 96744

Laie Hawaii Stake
Branch Genealogy Library
BYU - Hawaii Library
Laie, Hawaii 96762

IDAHO

Bear Lake Branch Genealogy
Library
Bear Lake County Library
138 North 6th Street
Montpelier, Idaho 83254

Blackfoot Idaho West Stake
Branch Genealogy Library
Stake Center
6 mi. N.W. of Blackfoot
on Pioneer Road,
Idaho 83221

Boise Idaho Branch
Genealogy Library
325 State Street
Boise, Idaho 83702

Burley Idaho Branch
Genealogy Library
224 E. 14th Street
Burley, Idaho 83318

Driggs Idaho Stake
Branch Genealogy Library
Stake Center
221 North 1st East
Driggs, Idaho 83422

Idaho Falls Idaho
Branch Genealogy Library
290 Chestnut Street
Idaho Falls, Idaho 83401

Iona Idaho Stake
Branch Genealogy Library
Stake Center
Iona, Idaho 83427
                    PROPOSED

Lewiston Idaho Stake
Branch Genealogy Library
Lewiston Idaho Stake
Center
9th & Preston
Lewiston, Idaho 83501

Malad Idaho Stake
Branch Genealogy Library
400 North 200 West
Malad, Idaho 83252

Moore Idaho Branch
Genealogy Library
Lost River Stake Center
Moore, Idaho 83255

Pocatello Idaho Branch
Genealogy Library
156-1/2 South 6th Avenue
Pocatello, Idaho 83201

Salmon Idaho Stake
Branch Genealogy Library
Salmon River Stake Center
Salmon, Idaho 83467

Twin Falls Idaho Branch
Genealogy Library
Maurice Street North
Twin Falls, Idaho 83301

Upper Snake River
Branch Genealogy Library
Ricks College Library
Rexburg, Idaho 83440

ILLINOIS

Champaign Illinois Stake
Branch Genealogy Library
Illinois Stake Center
604 West Windsor Road
Champaign, Illinois 61820

Chicago Heights Illinois
Stake Branch Genealogy
Library
402 Longwood Drive
Chicago Heights, Illinois
60430

Naperville Illinois Stake
Branch Genealogy Library
Stake Center
24 W341 Chicago Avenue
Naperville, Illinois 60540

Wilmette Illinois
Branch Genealogy Library
2801 Lake Avenue
Wilmette, Illinois 60091

INDIANA

Ft. Wayne Indiana Stake
Branch Genealogy Library
5401 St. Joe Road
Ft. Wayne, Indiana 46804

Indianapolis Indiana
Branch Genealogy Library
Stake Center
900 East Stop 11 Road
Indianapolis, Indiana 46227

IOWA

Des Moines Iowa Stake
Branch Genealogy Library
3301 Ashworth Road
West Des Moines, Iowa 50265

KANSAS

Wichita Kansas Stake
Branch Genealogy Library
Stake Center
7011 East 13th Street
Wichita, Kansas 67206

KENTUCKY

Lexington Kentucky Stake
Branch Genealogy Library
Stake Center
Lexington, Kentucky 40503
PROPOSED

LOUISIANA

Baton Rouge Louisiana
Branch Genealogy Library
5686 Winbourne Avenue
Baton Rouge, Louisiana
70803

MAINE

Augusta Maine Stake
Branch Genealogy Library
Augusta Ward Chapel
Hasson Street
Farmingdale, Maine 04330

MARYLAND

Silver Spring Maryland
Branch Genealogy Library
500 Randolph Road
Silver Spring, Maryland
20904

MASSACHUSETTS

Boston Massachusetts
Stake Branch Genealogy
Library
Brown Street & South Avenue
Weston, Massachusetts 02193

MEXICO

Colonia Juarez Mexico
Stake Branch Genealogy
Library
Colonia Juarez
Chihuahua, Mexico

Mexico City Mexico
Branch Genealogy Library
Churu Busco Stake Center
Mexico City, Mexico

MICHIGAN

Bloomfield Hills Michigan
Stake Branch Genealogy
Library
425 No. Woodward Avenue
Bloomfield Hills, Michigan
48013

Dearborn Michigan Stake
Branch Genealogy Library
Dearborn Michigan Chapel
20201 Rotunda Drive
Dearborn, Michigan 48124

Lansing Michigan Stake
Branch Genealogy Library
Stake Center
431 E. Saginaw Street
East Lansing, Michigan
48933

Midland Michigan Stake
Branch Genealogy Library
Mid-Michigan Stake Center
1700 West Sugnut Road
Midland, Michigan 48640

Minneapolis Minnesota Stake
Branch Genealogy Library
2801 Douglas Drive N.
Minneapolis, Minnesota
55422

MISSISSIPPI

Hattiesburg Mississippi Stake
Branch Genealogy Library
Stake Center
U.S. 11 South
Hattiesburg, Mississippi
39401

MISSOURI

Columbia Missouri Stake
Branch Genealogy Library
Highway 36 South
Columbia, Missouri 65201

Kansas City Missouri
Branch Genealogy Library
8144 Holmes
Kansas City, Missouri 64131

Springfield Missouri Stake
Branch Genealogy Library
Stake Center
1322 South Campbell
Springfield, Missouri 65802

St. Louis Missouri Stake
Branch Genealogy Library
1239 Elizabeth
Ferguson, Missouri 63135

MONTANA

Billings Montana Stake
Branch Genealogy Library
1711 Sixth Street West
Billings, Montana 59102

Butte Montana Stake
Branch Genealogy Library
Dillon Chapel
715 E. Bannock Street
Dillon, Montana 59725

Great Falls Montana Stake
Branch Genealogy Library
1401 9th St., N.W.
Great Falls, Montana 59404

Helena Montana Stake
Branch Genealogy Library
Helena Stake Center
1610 E. 6th Avenue
Helena, Montana 59601

Kalispell Montana Stake
Branch Genealogy Library
Buffalo Hill
Kalispell, Montana 59901

Missoula Montana Stake
Branch Genealogy Library
3201 Bancroft Street
Missoula, Montana 59801

NEBRASKA

Omaha Nebraska
Branch Genealogy Library
11027 Martha Street
Omaha, Nebraska 68144

NEVADA

Ely Nevada Stake
Branch Genealogy Library
Ely Stake Center
Avenue E & Ninth Street
Ely, Nevada 89301

Fallon Nevada Stake
Branch Genealogy Library
750 West Richards Street
Fallon, Nevada 89406

Las Vegas Nevada
Branch Genealogy Library
509 S. Ninth Street
Las Vegas, Nevada 89101

Reno Nevada Branch
Genealogy Library
Washoe Public Library
301 S. Center
Reno, Nevada 89501

NEW HAMPSHIRE

Manchester New Hampshire
Stake Branch Genealogy
Library
105 Windsong Avenue
Manchester, New Hampshire
03104
                    PROPOSED

NEW JERSEY

Caldwell New Jersey
Branch Genealogy Library
Short Hills Ward
140 White Oak Ridge Road
Summit, New Jersey 07901

East Brunswick New Jersey
Branch Genealogy Library
303 Dunham's Corner Road
East Brunswick, New Jersey
08816

NEW MEXICO

Albuquerque New Mexico
Branch Genealogy Library
5709 Haines Avenue N.E.
Albuquerque, New Mexico
87110

Farmington New Mexico
Branch Genealogy Library
400 West Apache
Farmington, New Mexico 87401

NEW YORK

Albany New York Stake
Branch Genealogy Library
411 Loudon Road
Loudonville, New York 12211

Buffalo New York Stake
Branch Genealogy Library
PROPOSED

Ithaca New York Stake
Branch Genealogy Library
305 Murray Hill Road
Vestal, New York 13850

New York New York Stake
Branch Genealogy Library
Two Lincoln Square
(3rd Floor)
Broadway at 65th Street
New York, New York 10023

Plainview New York Stake
Branch Genealogy Library
160 Washington Avenue
Plainview, New York 13137

Rochester New York Stake
Branch Genealogy Library
460 Kreag Road
Fairport, New York 14450

NEW ZEALAND

Auckland New Zealand
Branch Genealogy Library
No. 2 Scotia Pl.
Auckland Cl, New Zealand

Canterbury New Zealand
Dist.
Branch Genealogy Library
25 Fendalton Road
Christchurch, New Zealand

Temple View New Zealand
Branch Genealogy Library
Temple View
Hamilton, New Zealand

Wellington New Zealand
Stake
Branch Genealogy Library
Wellington Chapel
140 Moxham Avenue
Wellington, New Zealand

NORTH CAROLINA

Charlotte North Carolina
Stake Branch
Genealogy Library
3020 Hilliard Drive
Charlotte, North Carolina
28205

Raleigh North Carolina
Branch Genealogy Library
5100 Six Forks Road
Raleigh, North Carolina
27609

Kinston North Carolina Stake
Branch Genealogy Library
3006 Carey Road
Kinston, North Carolina
28501
PROPOSED

Wilmington North Carolina
Stake
Branch Genealogy Library
Stake Center
514 S. College Road
Wilmington, North Carolina
28401
PROPOSED

OHIO

Cincinnati Ohio Stake
Branch Genealogy Library
5505 Bosworth Place
Cincinnati, Ohio 45212

Cleveland Ohio Stake
Branch Genealogy Library
Stake Center
25000 Westwood Road
Westlake, Ohio 44145

Columbus Ohio Stake
Branch Genealogy Library
3646 Lieb Street
Columbus, Ohio 43214

Dayton Ohio Stake
Branch Genealogy Library
1500 Shiloh Springs Road
Dayton, Ohio 45426

OKLAHOMA

Oklahoma City Oklahoma
Branch Genealogy Library
Oklahoma Stake Center
5020 N.W. 63d
Oklahoma City, Oklahoma
73132

Tulsa Oklahoma
Branch Genealogy Library
12110 E. 7th Street
Tulsa, Oklahoma 74128

OREGON

Beaverton Oregon
Branch Genealogy Library
10425 S.W. Beaverton
Hillsdale Highway
Beaverton, Oregon 97005

Bend Oregon Stake
Branch Genealogy Library
Stake Center
1260 Thompson Drive
Bend, Oregon 97701
PROPOSED

Coos Bay Oregon Stake
Branch Genealogy Library
Stake Center
3950 Sherman Avenue
North Bend, Oregon 97459

Corvallis Oregon Stake
Branch Genealogy Library
4141 N.W. Harrison
Corvallis, Oregon 97330

Eugene Oregon Stake
Branch Genealogy Library
3550 West 18th Street
Eugene, Oregon 97402

Gresham Oregon Stake
Branch Genealogy Library
Stake Center
3500 S.E. 182d
Gresham, Oregon 97030
PROPOSED

LaGrande Oregon Stake
Branch Genealogy Library
Old Welfare Bldg.
2504 N. Fir
LaGrande, Oregon 97850

Medford Oregon Stake
Branch Genealogy Library
2900 Juanipero Way
Medford, Oregon 97501

Nyssa Oregon Stake
Branch Genealogy Library
West Alberta Avenue
Nyssa, Oregon 97913

Branch Genealogical Libraries

Portland Oregon Stake
Branch Genealogy Library
2931 S.E. Harrison
Portland, Oregon 97214

Portland Oregon East
Branch Genealogy Library
Portland 8 and 14 Wards
2215 N.E. 106th Street
Portland, Oregon 97225

Salem Oregon Stake
Branch Genealogy Library
4550 Lone Oak S.E.
Salem, Oregon 97302

PENNSYLVANIA

Philadelphia Pennsylvania
Stake Branch
Genealogy Library
Pennsylvania Stake Center
721 Paxon Hollow Road
Broomall, Pennsylvania 19008

Gettysburg Pennsylvania Stake
Branch Genealogy Library
2100 Hollywood Drive
York, Pennsylvania 17403
            PROPOSED

State College Pennsylvania
District
Branch Genealogy Library
State College Branch
Whitehall Road
State College, Pennsylvania
16801
            PROPOSED

SOUTH AFRICA

Johannesburg South Africa
Branch Genealogy Library
1 Hunter Street
Highlands
Johannesburg, South Africa
            PROPOSED

SOUTH CAROLINA

Columbia South Carolina
Branch Genealogy Library
4440 Ft. Jackson Boulevard
Columbia, South Carolina
39206

TENNESSEE

Knoxville Tennessee Stake
Branch Genealogy Library
400 Kendall Road
Knoxville, Tennessee 37922

Memphis Tennessee Stake
Branch Genealogy Library
4520 Winchester Road
Memphis, Tennessee 38118

Nashville Tennessee Stake
Branch Genealogy Library
107 Twin Hills Drive
Madison, Tennessee 37115
            PROPOSED

Tennessee South District
Branch Genealogy Library
Old Shelbyville Highway
Tullahoma, Tennessee 37388

TEXAS

Austin Texas Stake
Branch Genealogy Library
Austin 1,2,3 Wards
2111 Parker Lane
Austin, Texas 78741

Beaumont Texas Stake
Branch Genealogy Library
Williamson Ward Chapel
Vidor, Texas 77662

Corpus Christi Texas Stake
Branch Genealogy Library
505 N. Mesquite Street
Corpus Christi, Texas 78401

Dallas Texas
Branch Genealogy Library
616 W. Keist Boulevard
Dallas, Texas 75233

Dallas Texas North Stake
Branch Genealogy Library
                    PROPOSED

El Paso Texas Stake
Branch Genealogy Library
3651 Douglas Avenue
El Paso, Texas 79903

Ft. Worth Texas Stake
Branch Genealogy Library
Ft. Worth Stake Center
4401 N.E. Loop 820
North Richland Hills, Texas
76118

Houston Texas Stake
Branch Genealogy Library
1001 Bering Drive
Houston, Texas 77003

Houston Texas East Stake
Branch Genealogy Library
Houston Stake Center
3000 Broadway
Houston, Texas 77017

Longview Texas Stake
Branch Genealogy Library
End of West Pine Street
Gilmer, Texas 75644

Odessa Texas Stake
Branch Genealogy Library
Stake Center
2011 Washington
Odessa, Texas 79760

San Antonio Texas Stake
Branch Genealogy Library
San Antonio Stake Center
2103 St. Cloud
San Antonio, Texas 78228

UTAH

Beaver Utah Stake
Branch Genealogy Library

15 North 100 West
Beaver, Utah 84713

Brigham City Utah South
Branch Genealogy Library
865 So. 3rd West
Brigham City, Utah 84302

Cache Branch Genealogy
Library
50 North Main
Logan, Utah 84321

Cedar City Utah
Branch Genealogy Library
256 South 900 West
Cedar City, Utah 84720
                    PROPOSED

Delta Utah
Branch Genealogy Library
52 North 100 West
Delta, Utah 84624
                    PROPOSED

Duchesne Utah Stake
Branch Genealogy Library
Stake Center
Duchesne, Utah 84021

Heber City Utah
Branch Genealogy Library
RFD Center Creek
Heber City, Utah 84032
                    PROPOSED

Knab Utah Stake
Branch Genealogy Library
Kanab, Utah 84741

Monticello Utah Stake
Branch Genealogy Library
225 East 2nd North
Blanding, Utah 84511
                    PROPOSED

Mt. Pleasant Utah
Branch Genealogy Library
Mt. Pleasant Stake Center
Mt. Pleasant, Utah 84647

Ogden Utah Branch
Genealogy Library
339 21st Street
Ogden, Utah 84401

Price Utah Branch
Genealogy Library
85 East Fourth North
Price, Utah 84501

Richfield Utah Branch
Genealogy Library
91 South 2d West
Richfield, Utah 84701

Santaquin Utah Stake
Branch Genealogy Library
Stake Center
Santaquin, Utah 84655

South Jordan Utah Stake
Branch Genealogy Library
2450 W. 10400 South
South Jordan, Utah 84065

St. George Utah
Branch Genealogy Library
401 South 400 East
St. George, Utah 84770

Springville Utah Branch
Genealogy Library
245 South 600 East
Springville, Utah 84663

Utah Valley Branch
Genealogy Library
40 HBL Library
Brigham Young University
Provo, Utah 84601

Uintah Basin Branch
Genealogy Library
(Old Jr. High Seminary
Bldg.)
613 West 2d South
Vernal, Utah 84078

VIRGINIA

Annandale Virginia
Branch Genealogy Library
3900 Howard Street
Annandale, Virginia 22003

Norfolk Virginia Stake
Branch Genealogy Library
4760 Princess Anne Road
Virginia Beach, Virginia
23462

Oakton Virginia Stake
Branch Genealogy Library
Stake Center
Hunter Mill Road
Oakton, Virginia 22124

Richmond Virginia Stake
Branch Genealogy Library
5600 Monument Avenue
Richmond, Virginia 23226

WALES

Merthyr Tydfil Wales
Stake Branch Genealogy
Library
Top of Nantygwenith St.
Georgetown
Merthyr Tydfil, Wales
                    PROPOSED

WASHINGTON

Bellevue Washington
Branch Genealogy Library
10675 N.E. 20th Street
Bellevue, Washington 98004

Bremerton Washington Stake
Branch Genealogy Library
2225 Perry Avenue
Bremerton, Washington 98310

Everett Washington Stake
Branch Genealogy Library
Everett Stake Center
Everett, Washington 98201

Longview Washington Stake
Branch Genealogy Library
1721 30th Avenue
Longview, Washington 98632

Moses Lake Washington Stake
Branch Genealogy Library
1515 Division
Moses Lake, Washington
98837

Mt. Vernon Washington
Branch Genealogy Library
1700 Hazel
Mt. Vernon, Washington
98273

Olympia Washington Stake
Branch Genealogy Library
Olympia Stake Center
Olympia, Washington 98503

Pasco Washington Stake
Branch Genealogy Library
Pasco Stake Center
2004 N. 24th Street
Pasco, Washington 99301

Quincy Washington Stake
Branch Genealogy Library
1101 2d South East
Quincy, Washington 98824

Richland Washington Stake
Branch Genealogy Library
1720 Thayer Drive
Richland, Washington 99352

Seattle Washington North
Stake Branch Genealogy
Library
Stake Center
5701 8th N.E.
Seattle, Washington 98115

Spokane Washington
Branch Genealogy Library
N. 919 Pines Road
Spokane, Washington 99206

Tacoma Washington
Branch Genealogy Library
South 12th and Pearl Street
Tacoma, Washington 98466

Yakima Washington Stake
Branch Genealogy Library
705 S. 38th Avenue
Yakima, Washington 98901

WISCONSIN

Milwaukee Wisconsin Stake
Branch Genealogy Library
Stake Center
9600 W. Grange Avenue
Hales Corner, Wisconsin
53130

Appleton Wisconsin Dist.
Branch Genealogy Library
Lodge Hall
Main Street
Shawano, Wisconsin 54166

WYOMING

Afton Wyoming Stake
Branch Genealogy Library
347 Jefferson
Afton, Wyoming 83110

Casper Wyoming Stake
Branch Genealogy Library
Stake Center
700 S. Missouri
Casper, Wyoming 82602

Cheyenne Wyoming Stake
Branch Genealogy Library
Wyoming County Library
2800 Central Avenue
Cheyenne, Wyoming 82001

Cody Wyoming Branch
Genealogy Library
Cody Ward Chapel
Cody, Wyoming 82414

Evanston Wyoming Stake
Branch Genealogy Library
1224 Morse Lee Street
Evanston, Wyoming 82930

Lovell Wyoming Stake
Branch Genealogy Library
Stake Center
50 West Main
Lovell, Wyoming 82431

INDEX

This index is alphabetized letter by letter. Underscored numbers refer to main areas within subjects.

A

Abbreviations (Zkratky) 149
 in matriky and documents
  124-26
 of the names of churches
  44
Abeceda. See Alphabet, Czech
  and Slovak
Administrative Districts
  (Kraj, Oblast)
 establishment of 15
 list of 62-71
 map of 63
Alphabet, Czech and Slovak
  (Česká Abeceda) 122-24
 in alphabetizing 17, 62
 modernization of 82
Anabaptists in Moravia 58
Ancestral residence 16-17
Apostolic Vicariat, Vienna
  51
Archival Guides (Průvodce po
  Archívech) 73
Archival Publications 73-77
Archives 61-77
 city 76-77
 classification of 61
 county 75-76
 district 72-73
 estates 50, 52, 55, 61
 sample entries of 72
 state 73-74, 75
 See also Archival Guides;
  Archival Publications
Armorials (Erbovníci) 151.
  See also Heraldry; No-
  bility
ARTIA (book dealer) xiii,
  154

Austria
 biographic dictionary of
  161
 empire 15-16
 people of 16

B

Battle of White Mountain.
  See White Mountain,
  Battle of
Berní Rula. See Tax Lists
Bethlehem, Pennsylvania 26
Bílá Hora. See White Moun-
  tain, Battle of
Biographies of Czechs and
  Slovaks in United States
  35
Bohemia
 castles and fortresses of
  161
 Czech nation in 12
 early maps of 21-22
 eighteenth century 11
 history of crafts and com-
  merce in 58
 Jews in 43-44
 kingdom of 5-9
  map of 6
 map of Duchy of 7
 as a province of Czechoslo-
  vakia 15
 refugees from 35
 South 10
 See also Bohemians in
  America; Czechoslovakia;
  Czechs in America
Bohemian Brethren (Bratrská
  Jednota) 7-8

181

Index

Index